BUILD IT AND THEY WILL COME

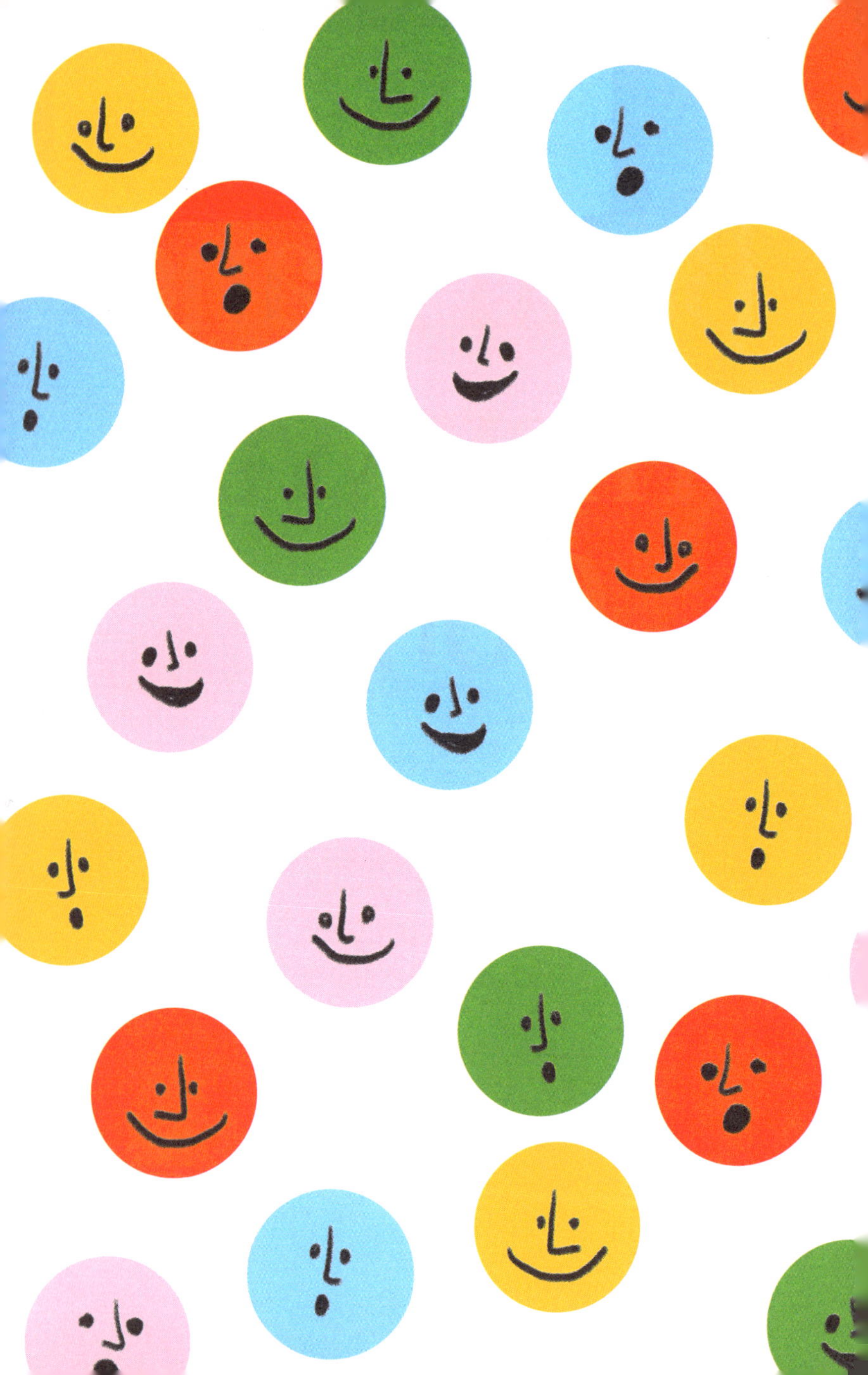

Build It and They Will Come

A Guide to Architecting Intentional Community

CAT LANTIGUA

parea
BOOKS

*To Guela, Tia Carmen,
and the Bronx*

CONTENTS

PREFACE vii
INTRODUCTION xiii

PART ONE Design 1

CHAPTER ONE *Belonging* 3

CHAPTER TWO *Goddess Council* 24

CHAPTER THREE *Your "Why"* 48

CHAPTER FOUR *Culture* 57

PART TWO Sustainability 73

CHAPTER FIVE *Disarming/Safety* 75

CHAPTER SIX *Leadership* 87

CHAPTER SEVEN *Money* 97

CHAPTER EIGHT *Burnout* 111

CONCLUSION 119
RECOMMENDED READING 125
NOTES 126
GODDESS COUNCIL HOST HANDBOOK 129
ACKNOWLEDGMENTS 144
ABOUT THE AUTHOR 147

"You Change.
All that you Change
Changes you.
The only lasting truth
Is Change.
God
Is Change."

—OCTAVIA BUTLER

PREFACE

I began writing this preface while visiting San Juan, Puerto Rico, one of the majestic islands that was home to my ancestors for centuries before our story began in the mainland United States. Throughout my trip I was awakened to previously unassessed levels of depth related to community, belonging, and resilience as I reacquainted myself with a culture I was not entirely familiar with, but have ancestral ties to. I engaged in long conversations with locals over my morning coffee and mallorcas, learned about the current social dynamics playing out on the island, ate as many traditional meals as possible, went to museums, and took in the symbols of history displayed everywhere. At some point, I was even mistakenly thought to be someone's cousin which, to me, was a sign that Puerto Rico was a place I could assimilate into with ease. The island and all of the beautiful people who live there inspired a feeling of oneness within me, which I hope to pour into this book, and ultimately into you.

If you picked up this book, it is because you are interested in learning how to bring people together and architect intentional communities. As you will soon observe, the word "architect" will come up often throughout the book. I use this word deliberately as a way to encourage us all to think of ourselves as designers. We are setting out to usher in the communities of the future, and if we want them to be sturdy and sustainable, we have to design their foundation with the same precision an architect brings to a building. There is no better time to honor your aspirations and to create the spaces that people are desperately in need of than the present. As someone committed to understanding the landscape of social wellness (and a millennial who came of age during the digital era), I cannot emphasize enough just how lonely our society has become. In the chapters that follow, I will get into the nitty-gritty details, but for now I want to emphasize that community building is the antidote to many of the issues affecting the health of our current social fabric. Therefore, any commitment you make to designing a niche and deliberate environment where people can safely unfold will have long-lasting, positive effects on the people directly benefiting from that environment, as well as anyone else they come in contact with outside of that dedicated space.

This book has been diligently written to serve as a community-building guide to empower anyone who yearns to impact the lives of others in a meaningful way. To tie it all together, I will share the personal experiences and deep-seated motivations that led me to this work. Beyond simply cultivating the skills needed to bring people together, the passion I feel about exploring the human desire to seek connection and experience belonging stems from a pocket within my soul to understand the human dynamics that have often left me feeling like an outcast. For as long as I can remember, I have always known that something about the way we all coexist could function better. My curiosities without a doubt spawned through my observations as a child in the Bronx, a borough in New York City known by many as a no-go zone due to its level of crime, inequality, and dilapidation (although through gentrification that has been changing a lot in recent years). I witnessed people who have been discarded by society try to navigate a world that was never designed to accommodate them, and I always wished there were more delicate and mindful approaches to how the cultures of the world developed to account for everyone's well-being.

At age five, I migrated with my mom to Miami where I completed all of my schooling, but throughout the years I took advantage of every opportunity to visit the Bronx. Although it was grittier than the suburb where I lived in Miami, the Bronx was home. Most of my family lived in the borough, and going back to see them always felt like home. At the age of twenty-four, I'd had enough yearning to go back home, so upon saving up enough money to make the move I returned to the Bronx. The part I wasn't aware of when I moved was that the prospects of making new friends as an adult, especially in a city of 8.4 million people, are usually slim to none, however there was an overpowering inclination within me to transmute my feelings of loneliness into manifesting the community I longed for. Along the way I naively (or maybe wisely . . . I am still not sure) used the internet as a way to do just that. Within a few years of being back in the city, I committed to an ethos of leading with vulnerability and authenticity as I shared my thoughts in a self-produced podcast, *Chats with Cat*; lengthy Instagram captions; blog posts; and most notably, by building the global women's community I chose to call Goddess Council. I had no idea what it would lead to, but now I have written this entire book detailing everything that happened after I dared to tell the world I was building the sisterhood I *needed*, and they were invited to join it.

My intention in writing this community architecting guide is to share the nuances, tips, and cautionary tales I wish someone had told me before I set out on the grand experiment of manifesting a sisterhood with the help of the internet. The guide is organized into two sections that will help us achieve three main objectives:

1. We will define and deepen our interpretation of the essence of community by analyzing your inspiration to bring people together, your "why," and what exactly you are seeking to offer the world, your mission. We will also explore my personal tenets, how Goddess Council came to be, and critiques on the modern social constructs that are exacerbating feelings of loneliness and isolation. The goal is to prompt you with questions and perspectives that will usher you into a feeling of confidence in your ability to architect something in real life that has not been done before while honoring your heart's truest desire and intuitive vision.
2. We will explore the fundamentals of how to intentionally architect a community by unpacking themes around culture, community safety, inclusivity, leadership, and financial sustainability. The objective throughout this section is to analyze proposed considerations that I believe can fortify sustainable and grounded community success.
3. Additionally, we will hone in on my proposed non-negotiables and elements that I implore should always remain front of mind in any community landscape. The objective is to pass on personal noticings and missteps I have taken in the past as a way to hopefully deter you from repeating similar outcomes along your journey.

This book is for deep feelers and anyone who is attuned to the communal needs of self and society. The safety of our future lies in our commitment to each other and our allegiance to our collective progress and togetherness. Some of us cannot help but notice, and be mobilized by, the energetic longings of both others and ourselves, and while that can often come across like a burden, I have come to appreciate it as a gift, and I hope you do too. Throughout many moments of my life I have wished that I wasn't prone to crying and emotional dysregulation when witnessing injustices. I have been made to feel unnecessarily disruptive when voicing my desire to live in a kinder world in the face of others who hold a resolute "it is what it is" attitude, but I can't help it—I'm just wired this way. On the other side of surviving a global pandemic and being shown the breadth of hyper-individualism's consequences, I have a newfound appreciation for my sensitivity aptitude. Now I know that caring deeply about others and wanting this world to be better is a sign that I'm supposed to do something about it. Those of us who haven't been bogged down by the status quo and continue to embody the aspiration of hope, fairness, and collective care are still tapped into the consciousness of humanity. It is something that we were all born with, but some have lost sight of it throughout their acclimatization in this oftentimes merciless world. Simply put, the ability to feel feelings despite all of the harshness is a blessing. It means you're still connected to the spirit of kindness.

I do not have all the answers, and it is important for me to tell you that. Navigating community needs during a delicate time in history requires a forward thinking that demands multiple perspectives and solutions. My lens is undoubtedly informed by my lived experience, which looks different than that of most people. With that said, if there are gaps or considerations that seem obvious to you that were not mentioned in this book, take that as a sign that your voice is needed in the conversation of modern-day community building.

Preface

Make us aware of what else is needed. I am just one person with a desire to continually learn, but naturally I am limited in my awareness about everything related to this topic. Alongside the power you and others have to offer, we are unstoppable.

Together we can build new worlds.

INTRODUCTION

Existing as a human being at this moment is complex. In many ways, as a collective, we are prospering in the realm of medicine, technology, space travel, the arts, and many other arenas that impact humanity; simultaneously, we are beginning to lose touch with the essence of humanity.

At the onset of this book, and our experience together, I want to practice radical honesty with you. The topic of togetherness and collective expansion remains at the crux of everything I care about most, so I would be remiss not to take this opportunity to share *everything* I have been contemplating over the years. It kind of feels like, if not now, when? More importantly, I feel that we have all found ourselves at a fork on the proverbial road. The existential paths in question are: Will we continue to allow society to unfold as is or will we choose to commit to one another and build a new earth? Either decision will lead us down fundamentally different paths, but as of right now, only time will reveal which choice we have made. I want you to know I am ready for the new, but it is impossible to do it alone. So if you are like me and ready to claim your role in reimagining a new society where we can access the peace, stability, justice, care, joy, sustainability, and love we all inherently yearn for, I invite you to join me.

This guide was born from a desire to share whatever wisdom I have learned about navigating feelings of loneliness, belonging, and community. More importantly, this book feels like one of the most effective ways I can channel my energy to inspire and awaken changemakers to acknowledge the call

Introduction

within them that is asking them to take up space and create the change we are all desperately in need of. As a thirty year old who has already witnessed degradation across so many realms of life here on earth, this book also serves as a plea to anyone who is called to be a conduit for healing, growth, and expansion—the time is now.

We need you.

Throughout this guide, my hope is to equip you with knowledge I wish I knew when I entered the world of community building. This is also my opportunity to acknowledge those of you who have for a long time felt the pull to lean into transformation, imagination, and newness. These underlying feelings are the antidote to the helplessness and despair that have enveloped so many among us, but with focused intention, love, and faith I have no doubt we have the capacity to mold this world into a reflection of the most vibrant elements of what it means to be human. Truth is, we are experiencing societal shifts at a pace that many of us are having a difficult time keeping up with. Every day we can log onto the internet and discover that something we once thought to be true suddenly is false. Whether that is learning about the dismantling of laws we accepted as permanent, climate change destroying trees that have been rooted for generations, or leaders we have looked up to for decades being charged for crimes we could have never imagined. Simply put, there is a lot going on all at once, and yet we are expected to continue being active members of our families, agreeable colleagues, and proactive members of society. This often leaves me to wonder, Are people okay? Well, beloved reader, as you will soon learn the answer to that is . . . no. As a collective, we are not well, and while I do not have all of the answers as to how to remedy the issues we are confronting, I know one thing: the only way through this is together. In the following chapters I will do my very best to equip you with the groundwork to feel empowered to impact the world around you.

I'm not sure if this book is off to the start you may have expected, but I would like to consider this guide as my Trojan horse.[1] Yes, we will get into the fundamental details of architecting intentional community, but my primary goal in creating this body of work is to awaken hope and faith that things can and will get better. All is not lost, however, as I will consistently remind you, we have to come back to one another if we are going to not only survive but also thrive.

I said I would be honest, so I cannot continue on without acknowledging that I have not always been this optimistic about our collective future. Part of what led me down the path of cynicism in the past was struggling with chronic loneliness, but also having grown into adulthood (along with my entire generation and Gen Z) during the unraveling of the digital era, and thus having witnessed the horrors taking place across the entire globe that have baked skepticism into our collective psyches. It is almost as if we are always waiting for the other shoe to drop, except that every time the shoe drops, another one magically appears. Of course, previous generations have not been spared from experiencing their own hardships. That cannot be denied. I just cannot help but highlight the combination of circumstances that many of us who are just entering adulthood have been forced to navigate because many of the folks in the previous generations seem committed to minimizing our voices. In the United States particularly, we are trying to keep up with sky-rocketing rent, record-high grocery prices, inaccessible health care, a minimum wage that has not adjusted to current-day inflation, chronic gun violence, student loan debt, and more. (Do not even get me started on how single folks are feeling about their dating prospects.) All of this, while millions of us are witnessing wars and unimaginable atrocities that we never agreed to, taking place across the world, on our phones . . . in 4k.

Unlike the approach many have taken in their well-intentioned attempts to mitigate the nihilistic undertone plaguing the younger generations, I refuse to tiptoe around the fact that *yes, this is a lot. This is not fair. We have inherited a world marred with the carelessness of those who came before us and have been left to fix it without any clear directions on how.* Part of the reason many of us feel despair is because it seems like the folks with the ability to transform broken systems are vehemently trying to convince us that we are overexaggerating, this is how things have always been, or even worse, that we are just weak. As I reflect on my early twenties and recall the moments of sheer panic about the world I was entering post-graduation—it felt like I was in a void. It did not at all appear to me that others were witnessing what I was, which left me feeling paranoid about whether I would ever find myself actively being a part of society in the profound way I yearned to; however, eventually my outlook began to shift to a way of being that transformed all previous feelings of gloom into empowerment.

My newfound hope began to take form as I contemplated on the theory that our souls choose to incarnate on this planet during specific moments in time as a way to learn lessons, evolve, and impact the trajectory of humanity. Upon stumbling on this theory, my immediate reaction was to reject it, as I empathized and considered all the people suffering on this planet. I thought *Why would they actively choose to suffer?* I cannot confidently say that this theory will resonate with each of you, but the simple consideration of "what if" allowed me to take my life more seriously and commit to at least trying to see what impact I could have here. This outlook is what led me to write this book, and since it is now in your hands, it seems like I may have been onto something. Maybe if you give it some thought, it could do the same for you. I have evolved my way of thinking to assume that everyone is inherently equipped with special gifts that, if alchemized, possess the energy required to transform the way we coexist. The challenge presents itself in that we are all tasked with acknowledging and making use of these gifts as we try to survive a relentlessly complicated society. Furthermore, these gifts cannot be drawn out of us on our own, we need the encouragement and mirroring of others to make us aware of what lies within ourselves. So, how exactly are we supposed to make this happen when we do not have access to these nurturing environments? Well, it seems like we are left with no other choice than to architect them ourselves.

Before we dive into the contents of this book, I want to offer you a brief overview of what to expect moving forward. Part 1 will explore overall design. The intention of these chapters is to equip you with a frame of reference that will open up space for you to learn about current societal chasms that have created an undeniable set of circumstances that would prove any of your future community-centric efforts advantageous for us all. Chapter 1 explores the concept of belonging and getting to the root of what community actually is. It also highlights some of my critiques regarding the manipulation and corrupting nature of corporations' attempts to lead consumers down a path of false unity and acceptance as a way to drive profits. Chapter 2 offers you insight into my personal journey of navigating loneliness. It also details my entry into grassroots community building and my story about how I accidentally ended up founding Goddess Council (GC), a global women's wellness organization, out of my desperation to make friends in a new city. Chapter 3 is all about how to answer the call within yourself to become a community leader by guiding you to investigate your true underlying intentions while also assisting you to understand the responsibility that comes with assuming the role of someone others look to for hope. Chapter 4 delineates my perspectives when it comes to considerations you should make when conceptualizing the culture of your community.

Part 2 offers direct guidance in terms of elements that create sustainability while you actively architect the community of your dreams. We will examine themes that will prompt forethought for the overall energy you are seeking to cultivate. Chapter 5 encourages emotional intelligence in leadership and outlines soft skills that can be used to assuage the anxieties that oftentimes present themselves for new community members. I will guide you as you create a code of ethics, manifesto, and/or contract to explicitly state what the community you are building stands for. Chapter 6 explores the question of what it means to be a great leader. This is where I will outline some of the leadership flaws I came to recognize too late as a way to hopefully prevent you from making the same mistakes I did. Chapter 7 will delve into the role money plays in how your community will be able to access and achieve certain goals. Chapter 8 will analyze the meaning of burnout and delve into approaches that can prompt leaders to feel disillusioned or exhausted along their journey to create social change.

Finally, I will summarize lessons learned. I will offer questions to contemplate as you further your progress in architecting your community and will suggest community leaders you can turn to for further guidance and learning.

Okay, are you ready? Let us jump in.

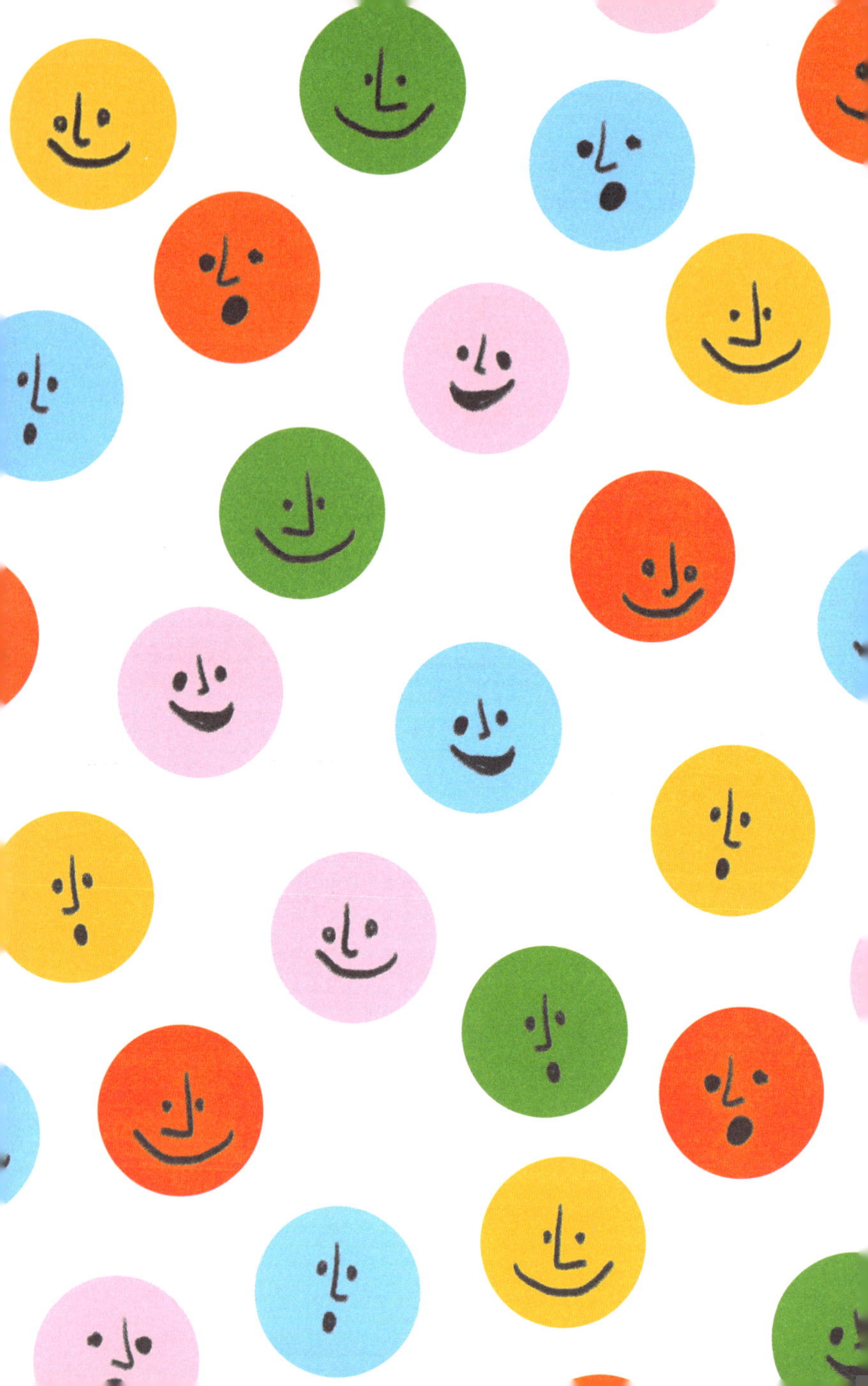

PART ONE
Design

CHAPTER ONE
Belonging 3

CHAPTER TWO
Goddess Council 24

CHAPTER THREE
Your "Why" 48

CHAPTER FOUR
Culture 57

CHAPTER ONE

Belonging

Community is home. It is the embodiment of the togetherness that helps us feel like we are a part of something bigger than our singular existence. I believe that the potential to experience the beauty of deep human bonds is why our souls chose to incarnate here on earth. The opportunity to feel seen, accepted, validated, supported, and cherished simply for being serves as the undercurrent of what inspires most humans to show up to life each day. So how did we get to a point in society where most of us do not feel like we have access to these kinds of bonds? How did we become such a lonely and isolated bunch? How do we expect ourselves to thrive and become our best selves if we do *not* feel a part of a more expansive consciousness?

Let me start off by acknowledging that navigating being a human these days is beyond tough. If I am being honest, it often feels like we are not all existing on the same planet. So many of the struggles we experience as a society stem from there being so many differences in opinion and staunchly held moral values that span across critically important realms of coexistence. As we witness governments squabble within and between each other, individually we attempt to thrive amid rising costs of living, higher unemployment rates, climate change, and other challenges that have become increasingly impossible to ignore. I am not even slightly close to being able to offer foolproof solutions to our collective struggles, but I know one thing: to not only survive but also create solutions to the issues born out of late-stage capitalism, we need to access opportunities and spaces that offer reprieve. I cannot help but wonder, however, where exactly to find such a space if it has not presented itself by now?

This is something I have contemplated throughout my twenties. I have consciously (and unconsciously) obsessed over my general lack of community and attempted to unpack why I have left so many interactions feeling like all I wanted to do was run away. For starters, I have always been a highly sensitive person, which has led me to oftentimes feel like I was too complicated to be understood. This led me down a path of internal hypervigilance, where I eventually convinced myself that it would be easier if I just kept to myself. My first memory of this was when I was around six years old, after I had left behind most of my family in the Bronx as my mom and I started a new life in Miami. I was attending summer camp at the Boys and Girls Club of Miami, which organized a field trip to a skating rink for the age group above mine. Upon their return, news spread that one of the kids fell while skating and had an accident so terrible that the paramedics had to take him to the hospital. After learning the news, I began to cry hysterically, and one of my peers asked, "Are you even friends with him?" And I said, "No, but I am so sad." Quickly, I realized that my reaction seemed strange when someone asked, "Why are you crying for someone you don't even know?" Now, given the fact that I was six, I was not able to explain what I was feeling clearly enough to be understood, so the moment passed as everyone moved on, but even now at thirty years old, I will never forget what registered within me that day. I realized then that not everyone processes life the same, and the ways we relate to one another can be vastly different. That day, I began to question myself internally before responding around others, out of fear that I would be perceived as strange or too emotional. Eventually, this morphed into a way of being that led me to emotionally shut down when I harbored a sea of sentiments, which became a point of tension in many of my future relationships until I unpacked it in therapy. Simply put, I have felt weird and out of place for many years of my life. Aside from apparently being too sensitive, as a child of the late '90s and early '00s, I grew up in an era where the media I was surrounded by shamelessly picked people apart, while simultaneously seldomly representing women and girls who looked like me positively. Over time, this gave me insecurities about my body that often led me to wonder if I was enough as I was. Eventually the confusing elements of the outside world creeped into my real-world experiences.

A specific moment that took place at a dance competition when I was in middle school marked one of my first moments of experiencing rejection, and subsequently altered the way I navigated my teenage years. During a quick rehearsal in a courtyard right outside of the main building, the team performed a choreographed dance to "Girls Just Wanna Have Fun" by Cyndi Lauper from start to finish. Despite the hundreds of times we had practiced prior to that day, our teacher wanted to be absolutely sure we could execute it perfectly. Tensions were high, and after we finished she started naming off different people who had thrown off our transitions. At some point in the midst of it all, she decided to yell out, "And Cat, you need to lay off the pizza!" in front of the entire team. I was in shock, and what followed was an awkward group of silent fourteen year olds looking at me with what seemed like secondhand embarrassment. After a few moments, I went on as if the comment did not affect me, but the shame I felt slowly snowballed into a vortex. In a moment of frustration, my dance teacher transformed my fourteen-year-old brain into a cozy home for my worst thoughts, but eventually I found an outlet where I did not feel worried about being judged . . . the internet.

By the time dial-up internet became a common amenity in homes around America, I was between graduating from middle school and entering the ninth grade. If there is anything I can remember vividly about those days, it is that being online was the most fun thing to do after school. Between downloading music from LimeWire, leaving comments on MySpace, and eventually chatting on AIM for hours, I was busy! As I think back on those years, I can recall a deep sense of community and belonging online. I would engage in lengthy chats with the different friends I had made outside of school, and often escaped feelings of loneliness because someone, somewhere, was always available. The internet at large also created a pathway for me to explore my creativity, which is when I felt the freeist. On most days, I was creating playlists and burning CDs for friends, getting lost on Tumblr for hours, and updating the code to update my weekly MySpace layout. Navigating social media and its modern-day implications drastically differ from what things were like twenty years ago. Before, social media platforms felt like judgment-free zones. Now, despite social media being integrated into most of our lives, it is impossible to deny that it is not as fun as it used to be. As I have heard throughout many conversations with folks across the millennial and Gen-Z spectrum, there is a growing feeling that many of the popular social media platforms are ruining the user experience with their ever-evolving algorithms and relentless ads. Simply put, people just want to feel connected.

THE ESSENCE OF COMMUNITY

At the core of my initiation into the world of community building is witnessing it up close within my family. For my family, who immigrated to the United States from the Dominican Republic and Puerto Rico, the possibility of survival in America was predicated on community support. They were received by the diaspora and quickly made to feel like they were home within an intense new microcosm. Being born in New York City, to very young parents, meant that my existence and well-being was also contingent on the strength of the community my family could rely on. I have memories of being looked after by members of the tight-knit network of aunts, uncles, cousins, and church friends who all played a role in forming me into the woman I am today. Without them, there would have been no chance for my parents to work or find their footing in a society that does not usually prioritize subsidizing childcare. I mention this all because I want you to know that when I use the word "community," I use it to describe the deepest essence of what the word points to.

The word "community" derives from the classical Latin word *commūnitās,* which is defined as "the very spirit of community; an intense community spirit, the feeling of great social equality, solidarity, and togetherness."[1] Although initially meant to describe something profound, in the modern context, I have noticed a pattern of the word "community" being used to describe loose ties and superficial connections. I suspect this is because many people crave the spirit of community but are not exactly familiar with what it looks and feels like. So, the word is used to describe something that hopes to serve as a community, but oftentimes lacks in its ability to actually deliver on the meaning of the word. Time and time again I have witnessed disillusionment from people who show up to events, networking opportunities, or gatherings under the guise that they will feel a sense of community, only to realize that was not the actual experience designed for them.

REAL CONNECTION, PLEASE

Like many of you, I have always been the kind of person who enters gatherings hoping to *really* feel something. To go beyond the small talk and be acknowledged for reasons beyond physical appearances or what I do for a living. I want to be asked meaningful questions that allow me to show up as my authentic self. The possibility of potentially making wholesome connections is what always inspires me to overcome my introversion and put myself out there, but more often than not, I leave interactions wanting to throw my head back and let out a guttural "UGHHHHHHHH" because, although I am showing up to a space that claims to be about fostering community, the strangers who fill up these rooms often replicate the sterile energy of networking engagements. At the end of these events, I am left feeling like my energy was expected to be transactional and my bland responses to ordinary questions make the real me imperceptible. I can recall going to events in New York and being asked the unoriginal "What do you do?" question, to which I responded with some version of "I work a day job that isn't very interesting but pays the bills. After work I self-produce a podcast called *Chats with Cat* and I write for my blog." As I would say this, I would catch people's eyes glazing over seemingly because at no point did I mention a recognizable company or "noteworthy" person. Over time, as Goddess Council became more of a "thing," its mention would catch the attention of some folks, but it still never felt enough for most people during our initial interactions. The folks trying to navigate networks in major cities like NYC, LA, Miami, or Atlanta can attest to this acute phenomenon of feeling like you're a means to an end for someone else to fulfill their personal agenda. Maybe it is just a by-product of living in big cities—which up until now has been my only experience—but I often felt like I only had a few moments to deliver an elevator pitch on what I do in the world, and during that time the other person would quickly determine if chatting with me was worthwhile; and if I was not interesting enough I would be subtly disregarded. In the moments where I was able to push through that awkward realization that the other person was losing interest in me, I would attempt to ask them questions like "How is your day going so far?" or "What fun hobbies have you been leaning into lately?" but to no avail. Their mind would already be wandering off to scope out who they wanted to talk to next. This did not just happen once or twice or even in one single city; this was and continues to be a common occurrence. What shocks me these days is that despite collectively experiencing the aftershocks of the pandemic in 2020, and learning how interconnected we all are in terms of our mutual survival, I am still confronted with superficial encounters. Oftentimes, I catch myself wondering if all along I have just been too naive to pick up on the cultural attitudes everyone else has agreed to. Like, am I missing something? Am I wrong for wanting more? Does this resonate with you? Surely, I am not the only one picking up on the lack of depth being offered . . . right?

Before we go any further, let us square away some definitions about belonging to ensure that we are on the same page because it is about to get *real*. "Belongingness" is defined as the quality or state of being an essential or important part of something.[2] Dr. Brené Brown defines it as the following: "Belonging is being part of something bigger than yourself. But it's also the courage to stand alone, and to belong to yourself above all else."[3] Now, the conundrum I have been relentlessly confronting over the past few years (and maybe you have, too) is wondering exactly *how* I am supposed to feel like I belong somewhere if most times after "putting myself out there," I am left feeling worse off than I did before? How can I feel comfortable and happy with a particular group of people if I cannot find those people?

It must be noted that prioritizing a true sense of belonging within ourselves is one of the most important commitments we can ever make. Once we find comfort in the confidence that we love and care for ourselves, we can be anywhere and still feel grounded. Additionally, there is something special to be said about being able to experience solitude and getting to know yourself without interference. With that in mind, in May 2023 the Surgeon General of the United States, Dr. Vivek Murthy, put out a new advisory informing the world that we were officially experiencing a full-blown loneliness epidemic. Do you know how serious things have to be for the government to actually acknowledge it?! Dr. Murthy urged everyone to prioritize creating networks where community and deep connection could thrive, saying:

> *We are called to build a movement to mend the social fabric of our nation. It will take all of us—individuals and families, schools and*

workplaces, health care and public health systems, technology companies, governments, faith organizations, and communities—working together to destigmatize loneliness and change our cultural and policy response to it. It will require reimagining the structures, policies, and programs that shape a community to best support the development of healthy relationships.

Each of us can start now, in our own lives, by strengthening our connections and relationships. Our individual relationships are an untapped resource—a source of healing hiding in plain sight. They can help us live healthier, more productive, and more fulfilled lives. Answer that phone call from a friend. Make time to share a meal. Listen without the distraction of your phone. Perform an act of service. Express yourself authentically. The keys to human connection are simple, but extraordinarily powerful.[4]

In addition to this recent advisory, a report from the National Academies of Sciences, Engineering, and Medicine (NASEM) points out that more than one-third of adults age forty-five and older feel lonely, and nearly one-fourth of adults age sixty-five and older are considered socially isolated.[5] Clearly, there is a disconnect among us, and when I think about how this will play out over the years—the increased health disadvantages such as cardiovascular disease, diabetes, and hypertension paired with the general lack of community interconnectedness that thrives in a society of isolated people—it overwhelms me. I cannot help but think about the gamut of experiences and advancements humanity will be missing out on because of our lack of commitment to communing with one another; progress that we will never be able to account for as it just does not exist.

To me, this has always felt heartbreaking.

WE ARE NOT MEANT TO LIVE LIFE ON OUR OWN

As I hold in tandem the definitions of *commūnitās* and belonging and the heightened state of loneliness spanning generations, I feel a sense of urgency. The health risks associated with social isolation are serious and impacting the lives of millions right now. Combating the adverse health implications of loneliness is not just a matter of finding ways to be surrounded by people who can be spoken to; it is also about engaging in meaningful bonds, and the body will intuitively know the difference. As I reflect on the ways that loneliness has impacted my own life, I am brought back to a moment in a recent therapy session where I recalled memories from my early days in Miami after leaving my safety net in the Bronx. As a six year old navigating a new environment, with a twenty-three-year-old mom who was trying her best to understand the mind of a highly sensitive child, I have flashbacks of being in my room feeling like I just did not want to be on this planet. I would quietly cry for hours alone in my room, wishing that I could go back to the cozy embrace of my Guela or to walk down the block of my old neighborhood knowing I would stumble across familiar faces. I wanted to be surrounded by people who looked like me and to walk around a place that felt like it understood the intersections of my existence. Even at such a young age I knew that something important was missing in my life, although I was unable to describe it. I am not sure what the impacts of that longing were on my barely formed brain, but I have no doubt it still impacts me to this day.

Consciously choosing to build an intentional community in this day and age should be taken as seriously as possible. Throughout this book we will get into the details of exactly how to do that, but I feel it is important to emphasize that many people are struggling both to stay afloat and to stay hopeful in our society. If you plan to send out the proverbial bat signal and give people hope that what you are building will embody the feeling of great social equality, solidarity, and togetherness—mean it! Community and connection are quite literally linked to life or death. The reality of the impact connection has on our bodies cannot be denied, but the scope of its importance spans even further than that. Being in community with others creates safety nets where people can access assistance during the most vulnerable moments of their lives, a need that continues to be exacerbated under the dire circumstances of modern times. An example that immediately comes to mind is the function of community fridges in underserved neighborhoods. As a result of the community at large freely filling up refrigerators, folks who would otherwise possibly starve can nourish their bodies.

    I saw this up close over the summer when I fundraised to fill four community fridges in Brooklyn. Less than twenty-four hours after filling them with staples, I went to check on the fridges and found them empty again. I felt mixed emotions. I felt satisfaction in knowing that I had directly contributed to ease in the lives of others, and conversely, I experienced discouragement that so many people are hungry and do not always have the means to sustain themselves. If I had not put food in those fridges that day, would those who benefited have otherwise not eaten? This is a consideration that my Guela planted in me from a young age, and I am forever grateful to her for encouraging me to recognize that not everyone has the same access to basic needs and that if we have means to share or secure resources for others, we should always go out of our way to help. Guela is so committed to this principle, that at least once per week, she stands in line at a local food bank to gather produce and pantry staples that she then distributes to those around the neighborhood whom she knows are limited in their mobility or struggling with health issues (she's basically an unofficial Meals on Wheels advocate). This is in addition to being a part of a network of folks who take turns cooking meals for unhoused people in the community every weekend.

Separately, the trend that I have noticed between Guela and those around her who embody the same mutual care practices is that all of them have in some way been affected by poverty or have had to make ends meet while marginalized. Even now, they don't have superfluous wealth, but the extra that they do have is put toward lifting those who have even less. When peering through an individualistic lens, one could imagine that anyone who hasn't had much would use the extra money that comes their way for themselves, but what Guela and others in the Bronx have taught me is that not everyone views life that way. Those who prioritize being a part of the lives of others within their web of connections profoundly care about those people's well-being. In the dynamics in communities like the one Guela has fostered with her neighbors and fellow churchgoers, there is an unspoken thread of selflessness that flows between everyone. To them, the affliction of one impacts the contentment of everyone, and vice versa. Everyone works toward doing whatever they can to maintain the homeostasis of the collective, and to me, this has served as one of the most consistently heartening observations throughout my life.

This is the manifestation of community support literally being linked to the survival of others, which often leads me to wonder, who would bring food to the elderly in Guela's community if it wasn't for her? Some of her neighbors have no living relatives left and are figuring out how to survive completely alone. If she didn't fill that gap, what would happen? It's terrifying to consider, because in the United States especially, there aren't many safety nets that people can consistently rely on. The hyper-independent nature of American society (and many others) makes clear through its policies and allocation of funds that if you don't have solutions to your own problems . . . you're on your own. This is one of the many reasons why not having community support is so detrimental, because, I don't know if you've noticed, but it's a dog-eat-dog world out there. On a lighter note, I am hopeful. The fact that you're reading these words and taking interest in architecting intentional communities is proof that solutions that will impact the world for the better are already underway. You are the reason that things are going to get better.

As I have been alluding to, I remember feeling like I unquestionably did not belong throughout my adolescent years. My mom and I moved from the Bronx to Miami, where although there was a diverse population, I was a confusing character to many. Being Afro-Latina during a time where the Afro-Latinx representation in the media could be counted on one hand, paved the way for me to experience microaggressions from teachers, students, and basically everywhere else. And remember, in the early aughts anti-Blackness was still going unchecked in the media, so many people said hurtful things out loud and were almost never held accountable. The general cultural attitude toward me by Latinx folks in Miami consistently left me feeling like an outsider. Recalling this is interesting, because if I were to ask my peers from back in those days whether they were able to recognize my uneasiness, they would likely say no because eventually I learned how to remain functional despite an, at times, icky environment. My ability to insulate the dread I often felt day-to-day as I maneuvered surroundings that did not reflect me chipped away at any hope I had that one day my reality would be different, but there was one example being set for me in Washington Heights, Manhattan, that proved my theory wrong: Mother Cabrini High School.

THE SISTERHOOD THAT GAVE ME HOPE

My aunt Evelyn, aka Tia Evi, is my mom's youngest sister. When my mom gave birth to me at the age of seventeen, Tia Evi was only ten years old, so while I am technically her niece our dynamic has always been more like that of sisters. The move to Miami was tough on our relationship because we were practically attached at the hip (I reflect back on this fondly, but my aunt might have some irritating memories of my obsession with her). But she was so diligent about calling and sending me mail that it did not feel like we were thousands of miles apart. One of the things I always loved hearing about was her vibrant social life back in the Bronx; I lived vicariously through her. Although my Guela has always been a strict Catholic mother, Tia Evi managed to make a ton of friends and I was always mesmerized by the simultaneously extroverted and comforting nature she exuded to everyone around her.

Tia Evi, along with most of my cousins, went to what always seemed to be the coolest all-girls high school of all time, Mother Cabrini. I realize it is a rarity to hear someone boasting about a Catholic private school because from what I have heard they are usually um . . . pretty dreadful? (No offense.) Mother Cabrini was different; it was Dominican sisterhood embodied. The school was founded in 1899 by Frances Xavier Cabrini and sponsored by the Missionary Sisters of the Sacred Heart of Jesus. It attracted students from across New York City, with most coming in from the boroughs of Manhattan and the Bronx.[6] In its earlier years, the student body was mostly Irish and Italian immigrants, but by the time my family reached its doors it was made up primarily of students from the Dominican Republic or of Dominican descent. As a young girl feeling lonely, misunderstood, and confused about her place in the world, knowing that a place like Mother Cabrini High School existed and that my aunt was *actually* having a great time there gave me hope for the future. It served as a tangible aspiration and led me to believe that maybe one day I too would experience a sisterhood that allowed me to be seen for who I really was. The school itself seemed to have done an amazing job of keeping students engaged and excited about showing up each day, but what really stood out to me was how everyone would come together after school. I was fascinated by how Mother Cabrini served as a container for relationships to be established, but Tia Evi and her crew seemed to have the most fun after the bell rang.

Guela's house was *the spot* after school. Guela worked in the cafeteria at the Holy Spirit Catholic Church private school, so she was almost always home by the time my aunt and her friends arrived. From what I know, the girls would fill up on the fresh homemade pastelitos that Guela would whip up, adding vibrancy to the apartment by boisterously recounting their school day. Tia Evi became the plug within her vast network of girlfriends because she taught herself the art of the Dominican blowout and would hook her friends up while they caught up on the latest *chisme* in her room.[7]

When I think back on my high school experience and especially how it contrasts to Tia Evi's, I cannot help but be grateful it is over because it legitimately felt like four years of torment. Although I have some great memories of those years, I did not at all feel the sisterhood energy of Mother Cabrini. Attending high school in Miami felt more like survival of the fittest, and although I survived, I did not leave unscathed.

GOING BEYOND THE BOUNDS OF SUPERFICIALITY

The experience of belonging is different for all of us. Only we know what we have been devoid of and how that has impacted the way we developed as individuals. Although counterintuitive, it is typically from that very place of lack that we can cultivate a vision to build community that serves as a soothing balm to that pain point. The axiom "your mess is your message" is spot on. We will dive into this theory deeper in chapter 3, but for now, I want to emphasize that it is very likely that you can feel your way into building an intentional community by imagining a space and experience that could have made an impact on your own life. Others can pick up on whether an experience has been designed from the heart, and from what I have gathered throughout my many conversations about this specifically, that is what people are desperate for but cannot find. Folks are tired of being marketed the access to a potential new community with what seems like perfect language, only to realize that they are showing up to environments that lack soul. This has increasingly become more of a point of contention for me throughout the pandemic. From my vantage point, companies, and people in general, recognized the need for community (as made obvious by the high volume of TikTok videos, articles, and content flowing in about it during the pandemic), and decided to just put some things together to appear like they were doing something to combat the need. In rushing through the process and only using logic (and the profit motive) to piece together their vision, the creators of these spaces lacked sincerity, resulting in something that seems cool on the outside but does not actually make a profound impact. Which begs the question: Is this what capitalism really believes matters? Is the modern-day reality that brands will do just enough to create the illusion of care as a means of acquiring new customers, but never actually make right with what they are promoting? If so, my response is that superficiality and belonging do not pair. They never have and they never will.

    Instagrammable conferences and pop-ups do not automatically equate to belonging. I cannot deny the pervasiveness of Instagram and online brands that have mastered marketing aesthetics, pivoting their companies to hosting in-person events that are more like in-person hubs for content creation. After attending a few of these new-agey events/conferences it has become clear that oftentimes so much focus is put into what these experiences will look like, that prioritizing the feeling guests will have becomes an afterthought. This prevailing occurrence is draining, and I am ready for it to be over. Community and belonging are not a product you can sell. It is not something that is simply pretty. Community and belonging are experienced through a humanity-first lens. It is one of the most sacred languages of the soul. In the modern context where capitalism seems to be at the core of almost everything, community care cannot be conflated with or diminished by the profit motive. When I contemplate this, I cannot help but wonder: What are the elements of our interconnectedness that are not for sale? What boundaries are we drawing within society to ensure the sanctity of true human connection is upheld? I am inherently protective over the hearts of the people longing for something they do not know how to create themselves, but would emphatically pour themselves into if it existed by way of someone else. I once heard that some people are cut out to be organizers and gatherers, while others just show up. Since learning this, it has become impossible to ignore how clear that plays out in life. Now, I understand that we are not all cut out to be organizers, but in the context of being in a community everyone can discern whether something feels like a safe place, both physically and energetically. Upon feeling secure and accepted by those around them, people who would not necessarily be considered the architects of a community can show up in their own unique ways, and *that* introduces magic into the community. We all have varying personality types, interests, and gifts, and when they all come together it creates a splendid potion of the best things about being human. Having witnessed the impact Goddess Council had on so many, I now have a deep understanding of how willing people are to contribute to efforts they feel are authentic, relatable, and aligned. I would argue that regardless of how exhausting maintaining day-to-day life can be, folks would muster up energy to show up for a community they cherish. Despite the fact that there is nothing passive about being an active community member, it *is* recharging. Unlike the taxing things we are required to do as life maintenance (e.g., working, running errands, paying bills, etc.), when we engage with others who feed our souls, we walk away from those moments fuller. Our ability to flourish within a community rejuvenates our sense of self, regenerates our confidence, and reinspires us to make the most out of our existence. So, if you are heeding the call within yourself to show up and create intentional pockets of care and collectivism, please understand the undertaking at hand. Do not make any promises that you cannot actually uphold.

SOCIAL MEDIA CHANGED EVERYTHING

As someone who grew up both pre- and post-internet, I would be remiss to not discuss how feelings of belonging play out online. Traditional media typically does not leave me feeling represented or understood, and let us be real, most nonwhite folks feel the same. However, when considering the platforms where communication and expression could take place, I have thoroughly enjoyed it. I cannot picture my middle school years without AOL Instant Messenger or high school without BlackBerry Messenger. Naturally, the progress from these forms of technology to social media outlets like Facebook and Twitter (now X, but I'll stick with Twitter), then to apps like Instagram, Snapchat, and TikTok have heightened the level of access people (and the culture at large) have to macro-society. All these platforms were launched as a way to connect people positively and to make it easier to exchange information and catch glimpses into the lives, opinions, and realities of others. This evolved so much that Twitter was at the center of information dissemination during the Arab Spring in 2011, only five years after it was founded. With all of this in mind, it is safe to admit that social media platforms have played a role in creating some of the greatest social schisms we face as a society today.

Social media has become a never-ending contradiction—the pros and cons list are on par with one another. On one hand, social media has opened up pathways for micro-communities to form organically. Whether you are a gamer, yoga enthusiast, podcaster, or someone who loves to crochet, you can without a doubt type some words into YouTube and immediately find people creating content that is relevant to your interests (and even more folks you can connect with in the comments). Social media makes it possible to have a community of "your people" online, regardless of where in the world you live, and that has been a saving grace for many. In its earlier years, Instagram was a simple yet effective platform to share and organically engage with the people you followed. These days, ad-filled feeds make it more difficult to do that, and the culture of social media at large has turned toward perpetuating a false perfection and away from the transparency that drew many of us in. As I reflect back on my twenties it is clear that without my early online connections, I would have never met some of my dearest friends today. Over the years, had I not followed certain blogs, Instagram pages, podcasts, and YouTube channels it would not have been possible to cultivate my sense of clarity around some of the life perspectives that have helped me become the person behind these pages. Through Instagram and Twitter I gained an audience who engaged with my blog posts and interviews and eventually gave me the confidence to write this book. It is worth pointing out that I originally joined Instagram in 2013 and Twitter in 2009, when neither of the platforms interrupted communication between its users with algorithms, ads, or membership upgrades. Aside from the early days of online chatrooms, to me, these were the glory days of social media. It felt like everyone was there to keep in touch with the people we knew in real life and make new friends based on common interests and opinions. Now, Instagram feels like a stale version of what it used to be and Twitter is overrun with bots. Simply put, social media is not what it used to be, and while I understand that growth and evolution are part of the process of any company, unfortunately even technological advancements originally created to bring us closer have taken a turn toward prioritizing profit over connection.

The feeling of interconnectedness in online interactions oftentimes feels exciting and inspiring. I would argue, however, that it is not a replacement for the most authentic forms of human connection. A person online cannot sit across from you and ask you how you are feeling while looking you in the eyes, nor can they give you a hug, march alongside you in a protest, sit next to you on the couch to watch a movie, or hold space as you cry. Online connections should be supplements to the relationships we have cultivated in-person over time. By choosing to exclusively connect online, there is an inherent forgoing of the most tender parts of human dynamics. It cannot be denied that making new friends these days is not easy, especially as adults, but it is a worthy pursuit. For most of human history, the meaning of being in community was straightforward and easy to parse out, but now it exists on a spectrum. It can be experienced online, but it is ultimately embodied in-person.

REFLECTION QUESTIONS

1. Explore your own definition of belonging. When do you feel most at home?
2. From your vantage point, how are we in our society struggling to remain connected and attuned to one another? What do you believe has caused this?

CHAPTER TWO

Goddess Council

Goddess Council (GC) was the four-year accelerator that taught me everything I know about architecting intentional communities. The irony of it all is that I never intended it to be so. In order for you to understand the perspectives I share in this book, it is imperative to give you the scoop on how I arrived here. All the lessons and wisdom I learned about modern-day community building derives from conversations and dynamics I witnessed unfold between hundreds of diverse women from around the world. In sharing my truth and opening up my doors, I accidentally tapped into the collective "sisterhood wound" and my life was never again the same. *Reflective Healing* defines the sisterhood wound as:

> *the pain, distrust, or dis-ease that many women feel when relating to other women. Jealousy, insecurity, cattiness, comparison, fear—these are all ways that the sister wound manifests itself in relationships with other women. Instead of viewing the other woman as a sister, we see her as an enemy, competition, or source of harm.*[1]

Throughout the endeavor of designing Goddess Council, it began to slowly dawn on me that I too had been living with an untreated sisterhood wound. I had to release old perspectives that were inhibiting my ability to forge deep connections with new women, while passing on that newfound awareness to the women around me who were also undergoing a similar un-learning process. In hindsight, maybe that was one of the things that made GC so special. It wasn't just an opportunity for women to gather and meet one another. Instead, it was a safe space to overhaul toxic thought patterns that had been getting in the way of accessing true sisterhood, a reexamination that, if fully embodied, impacted dynamics that transcended the connections made within the community and transformed lives. Although Goddess Council closed down in 2021, I have no doubt that it made an impact on the lives of many, and countless relationships forged within it; and because of that, it will exist for decades to come.

SHAKING THINGS UP

Before my twenty-fifth birthday I decided I was going to leave Miami, the city I was raised in, and move back to the Bronx. I was yearning for that feeling of oneness I had with New York City. I moved back into Guela's apartment, and for six months throughout the winter and spring, I worked remotely and did not interact with many people outside of my home. At some point, it dawned on me that I was not living the life I intended and I had to do something to shake things up. Soon after my epiphany, I moved into a small, one-bedroom apartment in Brooklyn and promised to really "put myself out there." During this time, I committed to recording weekly episodes of my podcast *Chats with Cat* as a way to document my never-ending quest to make sense of life, while paving the way for my soul's purpose to shine through. I recorded the show mostly as a form of catharsis. Every week I spoke into a mic and the message I recorded went into the ether. Not many people were listening, but it always seemed like another way to connect with the handful of people I regularly kept in touch with. Little did I know that my show would open up the chance for me to interview some of NYC's coolest humans.

Around this time, I found out about the Wing, a new women's coworking space / social club in DUMBO, and decided to apply. A few months later, I was accepted and began going every single day (even on the weekends). I was committed to meeting fellow members by attending most of the events and building strong relationships with the employees I encountered daily. I think most of the members just used the club as a spot outside their home to spend a few hours every week, but I was there at least forty hours a week. Since I was essentially creating an entirely new network for myself, the Wing was the only place I felt like I was actually making progress in fostering new connections. Any New Yorker will tell you, the moment you step onto the pavement, you are just like every other person in the city, and if you do not already have "your people," the city can make you feel lonely . . . very quickly. After a few months of this, I began to feel more content and was even interviewing guests I met at the Wing for my podcast. Despite all of the progress, I still knew it was not enough. I had a growing feeling that I wanted to experience deeper relationships because the brief encounters I engaged in every day just were not cutting it anymore. Aside from a few special connections, most of the conversations I had revolved around answering "What do you do?" and then briefly exchanging Instagram handles to engage in peripheral social maintenance in the future. It is important to note that I could barely even afford the club's membership. Although my pantry was at times bare, I convinced myself that my membership dues were a worthwhile investment since I would be surrounding myself with some of NYC's most inspiring women. The Wing ceased operations years ago, but when I think back on those years, I can see how it transformed my trajectory. I was coworking alongside artists and cultural tastemakers I never thought I would meet in real life. Beyond simply being surrounded by some of the city's most influential women, I was slowly being infused with a newfound confidence in myself as an artist and creator. Unknowingly, these women demonstrated much needed representation for the possibilities that were available to me should I choose to pursue them. As much as I felt inspired by the amazing things people around me were up to, I oftentimes felt like an outsider as I tried to navigate the intense privilege and access most of those women had. It became clear to me that I was likely one of the few people choosing to forgo an extra $100 in groceries every week in order to pay the membership dues. In retrospect, I realize not everyone would consider this a wise choice, but this just goes to prove how much someone is willing to sacrifice in order to feel like they are a part of something. This feeling of otherness had been floating around within me for a few weeks and then, as I attempted to get on the subway one Sunday afternoon, everything changed.

The day seemed perfect. It was a sunny fall day, and I was making my way back home after attending a wholesome event in Bed Stuy. I decided to multitask and call my mom while I made my way to the subway, and after a few blocks I finally arrived at my station. While on the phone with her, I entered the turnstile and proceeded down the stairs to my train line.

Before I continue with this story, I want to remind you that part of living in NYC is becoming somewhat numb to the grumblings of the environment and people around you. There is an undertone of hypervigilance as soon as you step outside of your walls but eventually it simmers down enough to make it possible to move around and live life. In other words, I was paying attention to everything around me, but not flinching at anything that seemed abnormal. Okay, now back to the story!

As I began descending the stairs I noticed someone at the bottom of the steps, directly parallel to me. Every time I moved in one direction he did too. As I neared him, I realized he was at least a foot taller than me and it was clear that he was mentally ill. There was no other direction I could go in and I had to catch that specific train to get home, so I put on my bravest face and once I got close enough I firmly said, "Stop!" For a few moments, he just towered over me and I legitimately did not know what would happen, but eventually he moved to the side. It was only after he moved that I realized that three dudes around my age had recorded the entire encounter in anticipation that I would be assaulted.

Something in me changed that day. As I write these words I still cannot discern what it was exactly about this situation that transformed me. Was it the lack of safety? Was it the realization that my potential assault was merely perceived as an opportunity to upload the next viral video? I am really not sure. I just know that something clicked. Somehow, I managed to keep my composure enough to avoid scaring my mom as she listened in on everything.

I can only describe what transpired next as some kind of fugue state. I cannot recall getting on or off the train. I do not remember walking into my building. I do not remember much about the eight hours after "the Incident." But what I can connect with, even to this day, is my anguish as it dawned on me just how lonely I actually felt. More than anything, I wanted to call up one of my besties and tell them what happened so they could help me calm down and then invite me to decompress over thirteen-dollar cocktails at an obscure bar in the neighborhood. But I did not have any friends who could offer the support I wanted. I was a lonely gal, in a lonely city, with so much love to give, but no one I could pour it into. It was with this energy and teary eyes that I opened up my laptop and began envisioning the community of women I wanted to attract to and manifest in my life. It became obvious that without a true community I could not embark on any of the grand plans I had for my life as a quintessential twentysomething—or any of the years after—because I had always pictured my future full of friends from different chapters of my life. I pondered what I would call my group chat of the friends I had yet to make, and the name Goddess Council came to mind out of nowhere—divinely planted by the muses of creativity and sisterhood.

THE ROLLOUT

Throughout the eight hours after the Incident, I oscillated between feeling rage, sadness, inspiration, and clarity. I channeled that energy into a visual presentation I planned to post on my personal Instagram. I wrote out my intentions and the words that best described the essence of the connections that I hoped would form within GC. I tried my best to let go of the overwhelming disappointment I felt toward society and avoided internalizing resentment. Although the Incident altered my naive perspective around the guarantees I assumed were present within our social fabric at large, on a deeper level I understood that it was a catalyst for my inner growth. Even as I sat at my desk frustrated and angry at the world, I typed away and connected with a part of me that I otherwise would not have coaxed out. I had to feel the severity of my loneliness and the harshness of the world in order to actually do something about it. Had the catalyst not been externally driven or as dramatic and frightening as this one, who knows how long I would have trudged around NYC without making any real changes. Life has an interesting way of doing things, huh?

My game plan to announce GC to the world was, in retrospect, rushed and amateur, but also earnest. I just wanted to put it out there as quickly as I could and begin alchemizing my recently incurred blow. So, with my heart racing and loving openness as my guiding compass, I sent it off into the digital ether. I posted the visuals I created and announced that I was hosting a BYOB potluck at my place; I invited any woman who resonated with what GC was about to join! At the time I had a few thousand folks in my audience, and since most of them were spread across different cities, they were not necessarily my target audience, but because the internet is so vast and interconnected, people in Miami who knew people in New York recirculated and shared the GC flier and it made its way to the right people. As a safety precaution, any woman who wanted to attend would have to DM me and I would scope out their profiles to make sure they were not creepers on the DL, since everything would take place in my home. On the day of the gathering, about ten people had RSVP'd to attend, but it rained and only four showed up.

I was already nervous AF because I was going to host strangers in my home and my social anxiety ramped through the roof, so I actually felt relieved to host a smaller group. The evening unfolded in the most beautiful way. We drank wine, I laid out light bites for everyone to munch on, and we talked nonstop for hours. I was able to vocalize how I felt living in NYC and in turn learned that it was a sentiment shared by everyone present. We had the opportunity to be seen, heard, and validated—elements of connection that often feel impossible when you do not have any friends in the concrete jungle. In many ways, the potluck felt magical and surreal. At some point it dawned on me that my seedling of an idea had actually evolved into a tangible experience I was able to share with others. Our few hours together were everything I had been yearning for. It was after this potluck that I confidently knew I had the power and potential to continue creating the experiences I longed for. The solution to my specific needs would come *from* me, not by waiting around for someone to create it *for* me. As it turned out, my amateur rollout strategy was good enough to attract women with compatible energy.

After posting recap photos from the first gathering on Instagram, I received DMs from people expressing interest in attending the next event I hosted. I had not actually given any thought to hosting another potluck any time soon, so the interest caught me by surprise. Next thing I knew, I organized another potluck for the following month at my place. Twenty RSVPs quickly poured in and thirteen women actually showed up (which by NYC standards is a lot because people can be very flaky) and in no time we were packed into my little living room like sardines. My once quiet apartment that had no frequent visitors filled with boisterous laughter, overflowing wine glasses, snacks, and joy. Folks sat on the couch and the floor, and others stood around chatting in the kitchen. The aroma of the lit candles and the combination of everyone's perfume created a concoction of coziness. It was fascinating to witness the interactions between everyone—women whom I had never met mingled with the few new people I had connected with in NYC, and girlfriends who lived in Miami and just happened to be in town also stopped by. The conversations splintered off into smaller groups but never seemed awkward. Somehow, everyone floated around and entered dialogue with one another at the perfect moment. By the time my guests headed out and I was left alone to process how great the evening was, I felt overwhelmed with pride. I could not believe that in under eight weeks, so many new people had stepped into my apartment after months of being mostly occupied by me and my lonely thoughts. Outside of the gatherings, I began nurturing relationships with most of the women who came through. Whether keeping in touch through DMs or coordinating to meet up for coffee, I now had options to actually hang out with people instead of just fantasizing about it.

During one of those casual hangout sessions, a few of the women I began bonding with through GC urged me to consider taking things up a notch and making Goddess Council "a thing." They shared how impactful the community had been for them and offered to help me strategize on how to host more gatherings. To be honest, I had not expected this at all because deep down it felt like I had already achieved what I set out to do. I knew enough women to fulfill the idea I initially had for the group chat. I did not feel any inclination to overcomplicate things by creating anything formal, but I knew it was worth considering. Goddess Council began taking on its own meaning for the different people who experienced its magic and at some point it became clear that I could not gatekeep the allure.

THE INCUBATION PERIOD

During the five months after the Incident, the women who encouraged GC's evolution and I met up every week to brainstorm the future of the GC community. After I logged out of my remote day job, on most Monday evenings we would meet up at the Wing or at someone's apartment to bounce ideas off one another. We amped each other's ideas and leaned into all of the possibilities the future held for our community; we homed in on the feeling that we were really onto something. I stopped perceiving this idea conceived on the other side of a scary life event as something to infantilize. Instead, I chose to pour all of my passion into building it into an official social wellness brand that specialized in hosting thoughtful gatherings with the primary mission to help women make new friends.

Goddess Council began to seem not only like an opportunity to impact the world in a positive way but also a path for me to make a name for myself and, in turn, make my family proud. It had the potential to be *the* thing I could hold up and show as proof that betting on myself and my ideas had been the right decision. I thought about the impression I could make on young girls who came from similar backgrounds, and who, like me, sought out representation but were rarely reflected in positions of leadership. The concept of GC was radical in that it created experiences that were energetic salves to heal the sisterhood wound within so many, including myself. GC did not reach millions of women, but it infused those who it did reach with positivity and hope, feelings that when combined inherently beget transformation within ourselves and thus in the world. As a team, we gained the confidence to host larger events and pooled our resources to lock in venue spaces free of charge. This was an opportunity to begin blending my personal interests with the offerings that could be made available to others. Our first gathering outside of my apartment was an astrology 101 workshop hosted at a creative studio deep in the heart of Bushwick. The owner of the studio had a connection to one of the people who I met with on Mondays and, upon hearing about the mission of GC, felt called to extend her support by allocating the use of the space for three hours, free of charge. Thanks to her generosity, the proceeds from the ten-dollar ticket covered the cost of snacks, drinks, and the facilitator fee. Even better was the fact that we collected $100 as profit, and with that money I decided to take things up a notch and turn the idea of GC into Goddess Council, LLC. Soon after the formation of the LLC, I happened to move into a larger apartment and soon began consistently hosting gatherings on a biweekly-ish basis.

The era of Goddess Council was blooming. Each and every gathering felt unique, yet similar. They were soulful, wise, electrifying, wholesome, and reminiscent of something that, as women, we were supposed to be doing all along, but had lost sight of. As guests trickled in, I would guide them to the snacks and drinks I'd made available in the kitchen and introduce them to those who were already present. Eventually, about thirty minutes after the official start time, we would sit—along with our provisions—and form a circle in the middle of the living room, as if there were a campfire keeping us warm. Maybe the way we sat together allowed us to tap into something ancient and reassuring, but in no time the thoughts that had been pent up inside were considerately let out by everyone present. For over two hours, women who initially started out as strangers would share their thoughts on anything and everything. Each gathering had a theme (e.g., exploring the importance of boundaries), but that always turned out to be just the tip of the iceberg. There was always so much more that needed to be shared aloud. After every one of those "campfire gatherings" I would go to bed feeling like I had just tapped into a divinely orchestrated ceremony. Although I was slowly entering the role of facilitator as each gathering in my home materialized, it felt like there was a primordial guiding energy helping to mold the experience. By the time each of our gatherings came to an end, guests would exchange contact information and coordinate a hang out. These connections manifested so beautifully that years later, a doula who had attended a gathering in my apartment assisted a woman, whom she had met there, through childbirth.

Despite feeling like so many things were going right for GC, somewhere along the way, I began to disagree about the future of the collective with the folks who had initially inspired me to expand. The details related to the unfortunate fragmentation among the group were varied. Some of the issues stemmed from interpersonal misunderstandings within the group, and others had to do with disagreements about who the community should be of service to. Ultimately, what started off as something that I thought everyone fundamentally understood became a point of contention and controversy. It agonized me to witness what felt like a fortified unit fragment into pieces, but I felt a fierce protective instinct over what GC had begun to represent for so many women, and I refused to divert from our original mission. Soon enough, I found myself managing the ins and outs of the community mostly on my own. I often contemplated giving up and felt like I had signed up for too big of an undertaking. I did not have much extra income to invest in hiring help, and ticket prices for gatherings were set simply to cover the cost of snacks and drinks. Aside from holding a nine-to-five job, producing *Chats with Cat* weekly, and maintaining a life, I took on all of the responsibilities that up until then were spread across a group of people (e.g., event concepting, responding to emails and DMs, maintaining updated fliers, listing the events online, creating a marketing strategy, writing copy for our website, etc.). There were some events that had no RSVPs, and in general, building momentum during a time where there were so many distractions in my personal life and in the world at large, proved to be advanced-level difficult. Despite all of the hardships, after months of exclusively hosting gatherings in NYC, we were blessed to find a host in Miami who was open to expanding the spirit of GC, and soon after we were even set to launch in LA, that is until March 2020 came along.

THE YEAR THAT CHANGED EVERYTHING

There are the present times, and then there are the before times. GC was growing steadily and we were beginning to reach audiences in more major cities. When the pandemic struck, all of the plans I had for the collective were immediately chucked. The world was forcefully put on pause, and the future was not at all clear. It was impossible to host our cornerstone in-person gatherings, but I knew I had to figure something out. Within a few weeks, people began talking openly about how isolated they felt, and the general condition of mental health for many deteriorated. I decided that GC would begin hosting free events on Zoom and attempted to recreate the vibe of the in-person sessions. I felt confident that we could recreate the same conversations virtually that we'd had when sitting across from one another, especially as we were all having a shared traumatic experience. Ironically, after I'd staunchly advocated against substituting digital communication for in-person conversations, I realized the future of Goddess Council exclusively depended on how well we brought people together online. I would facilitate and set the tone for the experiences, but everything else was out of my control since I could not share a physical space with everyone. I had faith that the right people would be drawn to the offering. The first virtual gathering took place in May 2020 and was a Soul Check-In Brunch, with the following invitation:

Amid the craziness, let's create space to connect and ask each other "How are you doing?" Our lovely GC member, Jennie, will be kicking off with a grounding meditation before we dive into our convo and food!

Join in virtually as we all catch up over brunch and embrace the power of community!

Rules:
1. Eat/drink along with us—our intention is to make this feel as real as possible.
2. Dress up—nobody ever shows up to brunch in PJs.
3. Show up on time.

This gathering will serve as an intentional way to check-in and meaningfully pause.

Not only will we eat some amazing food, but we'll get a chance to openly share how we're feeling, exchange insights, and as always, make divine connections with our local goddesses.

With a crazy week behind us, let's take this time to cultivate joy, self-care, and community!

MEETING ID WILL BE EMAILED TO YOU DIRECTLY AFTER YOU'VE RSVP'D

Quickly after posting the gathering, it collected forty RSVPs. It went exceptionally well, and I knew more virtual experiences needed to follow. Thus, on behalf of GC I began facilitating events practically every day after I logged out of my remote job. We hosted happy hours, more brunch check-ins, and even converted our in-person book club into a virtual one! One day during a happy hour, a friend and GC OG (original goddess, aka one of the women who attended in-person events regularly in the before times) suggested we host some kind of collective journaling event that we could do together in the mornings before work. Little did either of us know that this simple idea would soon become an essential part of the self-care practice of hundreds of women throughout the pandemic.

THE COLLECTIVE GLOW UP

During the winter of 2019, as I scrolled on Instagram, I stumbled upon an announcement from a body-positivity influencer I followed and whose posts I faithfully kept up with. It shared the details of a contest seeking to award organizations in the community that were women-led and impacting lives for the better. The application required a video submission explaining how the money would be allocated if awarded. Since this was pre-pandemic, my next goal for GC was to organize an in-person "self-care fair" in Brooklyn and Miami. Along with scheduled workshops, I wanted to bring plant-based restaurants, wellness practitioners, artisans, and healers together into one space. I envisioned this as an opportunity for women to nurture themselves and meet like-minded others. I knew I had to set aside time to write a video script and record myself, but since the deadline was weeks away I added the final submission date to my calendar and pushed it off. As the weeks passed, I got caught up in the busyness of life and forgot about the contest. Then, I received a ping on my phone from my calendar reminding me that the deadline to submit my application was in two hours. Initially, I thought there was no way that I could complete everything required to submit, but thanks to the encouragement and video editing assistance of a friend, I submitted my application with just minutes to spare. On a random afternoon in February 2020, I received an email informing me that GC was selected as the winner and was awarded a game-changing twenty-thousand-dollar grant, making GC and me part of the first cohort of #AerieChangemakers.

It appeared like a sign from the universe that what GC was up to mattered, and that the goodwill we were putting out in the world helped to attract goodness to our mission. The actual grant was paid out months after I received the initial email, and by the time it did, the world had transformed—and my plans for the community were entirely different. Nonetheless, seeing the money in an actual account finally allowed me to feel like I could begin to put effort toward the next step, and as I observed the continuing decline of mental health in so many, I knew I had no time to waste. GC's creative director (aka my cousin Ari, who built GC's entire visual brand alongside her demanding full-time job) and I ideated for months about what should come next and ultimately set forth to formally design our own online community platform, where all of the virtual events many had grown to love would exist as a part of a membership package and private community. The money we were able to keep after taxes eventually allowed me to pay the fees for the platform hosting our online community, set up a business website and email, and even purchase a new computer.

It also offered the company a financial cushion to pull from as business needs presented themselves in the future.

While I worked on the rollout of the membership community, I also facilitated about ten free virtual gatherings a month and tried my best to tailor them to what appeared to be the needs of those around me. As I am sure you can remember, 2020 was an unhinged year that basically left all of us, particularly Black folks, disturbed. Within my four walls, I was combatting existential anxiety due to the pandemic, an uptick of senseless murders in my neighborhood, and a misaligned nine-to-five job. Like most people in the world, I was not sure how my story would pan out, but my ability to throw myself into being of service to others and making them feel better became my main self-preservation strategy.

By the time August 2020 rolled around it became evident that I could no longer continue balancing everything I had taken on. I was quickly withering. After my therapist implored me that something had to give, and I had to face the reality of the situation, I quit my full-time job and fully dedicated myself to expanding Goddess Council's efforts. Within four weeks of quitting my job, Goddess Council's *official* private online network was born. We launched a forty-dollar monthly membership model, which included a programming calendar of over twenty-five monthly events. It included a private discussion board replete with an array of topics that members could engage in and opportunities to experience virtual wellness workshops led by teachers and facilitators from all over the world. For a while, I managed every aspect of running the business: administration, programming, marketing, member acquisition, and facilitating at least twenty events per month (yes, you read that right, *twenty*). It did not take long before I realized that I was engulfed in a sea of endless tasks, exhaustion, and pressure. I needed help.

By March 2021 the GC team had expanded to include a social media and community manager. We began to operate like a well-oiled machine and I began to breathe easier. As vaccinations became more readily accessible, our 120-plus members began coordinating their own city-specific in-person dates and parties. From my vantage point, the mission GC had set back in 2018 was in motion: adult women were genuinely making new friends. As a founder/CEO, I began to learn how to properly delegate to others and, in tandem, opened greater capacity within myself to envision more community offerings. After more than six months of shifting the GC community into a private virtual space and many solidifying bonds, it felt appropriate to conceptualize a formal IRL reunion that would serve as a meeting place for members from all over to finally hug the people they had been building relationships with for so long over Zoom. Given that we tried to maintain a reasonable monthly membership fee and that operating costs were so high (the money from the grant quickly dwindled over the months), I knew that we did not have enough money to begin the process of planning the reunion, so we set out to crowdfund $10,000!

Aside from managing the logistics of running the business, facilitating five times per week, managing a personal life in the midst of a pandemic, and moving to different states, the team and I set out to crowdfund money. Luckily, Goddess Council was selected as a winner of yet another contest hosted by a crowdfunding platform dedicated to amplifying women-owned businesses. As part of the contest, we won $1,000, which was directly applied to our crowdfunding campaign once it went live, along with a twelve-week crash course held by some of the platform's educators to help guide us through from campaign ideation to the official crowdfunding launch. Setting up the back end of our crowdfunding was not only tedious and time consuming, it was draining. Without the crowdfunding campaign, I was working an average of sixtyish hours per week, but with the crowdfunding launch in the mix, I was averaging about seventy-five hours. It would be an understatement to say that all I did was think about Goddess Council. I treated the community like it was a newborn baby and I was fully committed to ensuring it lived a great life.

After a few months of intense planning, team meetings, copywriting, and customizing a marketing strategy, the crowdfunding campaign was announced to the world. Naively, I thought we had finished the hardest part about the process, but honestly, that could not have been further from the truth. On one hand, part of my frustration stemmed from my ego having a hard time putting itself out there day after day for thirty days straight in hopes of encouraging people to donate money for the future of GC (fun fact: Did you know that on average a potential funder has to be marketed to seven times before committing to submit a contribution?). On the other, it just was not an intuitive process for me from a marketing perspective. Nonetheless, after lots of strategic effort from the entire team and the GC community at large, we successfully raised the $10,000. We still had a lot of work to do for the campaign, like sending out the merchandise we promised, while actually putting together our action plan to achieve the goals we set out to fund: primarily, a wellness retreat and reunion that would bring together members from all over the world to have fun, gather, and experience joy after such a treacherous experience living through the pandemic. But before the team and I could begin to organize formal plans, I started to sense that some things were coming undone within the morale of the community. It seemed to me that something had changed about how folks engaged with each other.

Soon I discovered that during a few of the member-organized parties/dates, some people had begun to show parts of themselves that were not made apparent over the years. Many of us had gotten to know each other over our Zoom gatherings. Generally when members spent time in-person, things went beautifully and were an extension of the great times we were having virtually, but now I understand that managing the equilibrium of a community is delicate upkeep. I had poured everything I could into learning how to become a skillful host and facilitator during our events, but once members began engaging with each other without a mediator to maintain harmonious flow, hurtful words and actions began to enter the fold, which convoluted group dynamics during the official virtual GC gatherings and within the platform in general. All of a sudden, members who had been our loudest supporters were canceling their memberships and many slowed down their engagement with our messaging feed.

As we will explore further in the next chapter, communicating and befriending folks online can oftentimes be the pathway to creating the feeling of belonging between people or within a group. The flip side of this, however, is that you can't fully assess the people on the other side of the screen as you can IRL. When engaging with someone in-person, you can observe their mannerisms, habits, body language, and public treatment of others. In doing this, it is easier to decide whether you are compatible with someone and want to continue fostering a relationship or cut it off. Due to the isolating nature of the pandemic, most of our members built connections and friendships virtually first, which made it difficult to notice glaring red flags in some of our members. Before long it became clear that some of the people in the community were not only out of alignment with the values GC espoused, but had even turned to verbal bullying. I learned about these instances weeks after they had occurred, which left me in a tough spot because the damage had already been done and the effects of it had seeped into the overall spirit of the community. It felt like I was in over my head. Up until that point, I had never experienced conflict among members and had not created a plan of action in the event such issues arose. I was so busy trying to make sure the business stayed afloat that I did not have the foresight to imagine this possibility. For years it appeared like everyone who was attracted to GC understood our mission, values, and rules for participating in the community. We wanted to be inclusive of all women who understood the sanctity of the collective, but it turned out that some members chose to intentionally subvert everything we stood for and exacerbate the sisterhood wound within a space that was actively trying to heal it. Once I became aware of the damage, I went into overdrive as I sought out counsel from therapists and lawyers in attempts to rectify and mend the fractured group dynamic. Many of the remedies they proposed required an intense revamp that I desperately tried to implement through member contracts, community meetings to verbally reinforce GC's ethics, therapist-led group sessions to unpack the harm that had been inflicted by bullying, and by terminating the membership of anyone who proved to be a threat to the well-being of the community.

Goddess Council was so tight knit that a betrayal of anyone directly impacted the energy and charisma of all. Personally,

I never imagined a reality where any member would go out of their way to harm anyone else, so as a founder and an innate optimist, I truly was not equipped enough in the realm of conflict resolution to salvage the despondency I was beginning to sense from members. The effects of the collective (including me) having to confront the fact that a community as loving and open as ours was still susceptible to sabotage were cataclysmic. Over time, fewer members began showing up to events, there was not as much engagement in our private messaging board, and no matter what tactics the team took to enhance the experience for members it simply was no longer the same. The trust was not there and to my absolute horror, the magic that had been brewing within our sisterhood for so many years was slowly fading away. Intuitively, I knew that I would likely have to make an incredibly difficult decision soon, but I held off as long as I could because I was aware that it would devastate a lot of people.

IT'S NEVER THE RIGHT TIME TO SAY GOODBYE

When you put something out in the world with only great intentions and it builds momentum because other people are positively impacted by it, the feeling is indescribable. It is as if the universe is conspiring to give life to your seedling of an idea and you have somehow hacked into an enchanting aspect of being human. There were countless times where I just had to pause and soak in the extraordinary connections I was witnessing take shape, life-changing breakthroughs that transpired in workshops, and opportunities that made their way to our collective. So, when I made the inescapable decision to close down Goddess Council, I felt the intense and reverberating impacts of what I had done in the essence of my spirit. It was unlike any breakup or heartbreak I had ever experienced. GC evolved from a sapling into a blossoming tree, and in choosing to close it I was essentially ripping it from the soil and burning it. After months of exhausting all possible solutions and experiencing several mental breakdowns, in November 2021, GC concluded and I dissolved the team. The crowdfunding money went toward taxes, fulfilling merchandise orders, paying each member of our team a thank you bonus, a donation to a NYC women's shelter, and a small payout to Ari and me. As I write this, I still cannot believe how quickly something I had poured thousands of hours into came apart. I received a great number of personal messages questioning my decision to close down the community, but as the person who brought the idea into the world, I knew what the truest intentions were for creating GC and those intentions were being strained, so in my eyes there was only one option.

Over two years have passed since this decision, and now, I feel a sense of completion. Many of the women who met through Goddess Council remain close friends and continue to enhance each other's lives to this day, which is confirmation that the thing I built ultimately served its purpose. Although the community began as a solution for my own troubles, it evolved into a space for others to feel less alone, and throughout my lowest moments post-breakup it has brought me solace. Ultimately, Goddess Council also paved the way for me to meet some of my best friends and now my life is rich with the love of sisterhood that I longed for back on the day of the Incident. Now, my community is a beautiful coalescence of women from different phases of my life, and I have the honor of being engulfed in the kind of love and support I used to daydream about. Despite witnessing the world transform in worrisome ways every day, knowing that I have a grounding force of sisters all over the world who can be counted on offers me the chance to experience long-lasting optimism.

They say people come into your life for a season and a reason. Goddess Council's season lasted for four years and existed during a time when people needed it the most. Now, it is simply a cherished memory that serves as a reminder of the possibilities within sisterhood and what can happen when strangers come together.

REFLECTION QUESTIONS

1. Do you have a moment that stands out in your memory that made clear that you yearn to experience more tight-knit connections and the support of a community? If so, what kind of encouragement did you desire? Is that yearning still present within you today?
2. Is there a project or endeavor that you've embraced in the past that you eventually had to part ways with? If so, what led you to make that decision and what lesson(s) did you take away from that experience of detaching?

CHAPTER THREE

Your "Why"

These days a quick search on the internet will prove just how many options there are for basically anything, but when it comes down to finding a community to join, it is not that simple. Sure, there are platforms that list events, workshops, parties, festivals, and so on. We need to be real though, how often will a person who does not know anyone feel comfortable showing up alone to something organized and promoted on the internet? Regardless of how extroverted you might be, you will inevitably feel some anxiety about not knowing exactly what you're getting yourself into. Questions will run through your mind like: Who will be there? Will people be friendly? Will they be in cliques? Will there be someone there to greet me? Will this just be one of those networking events where people just ask me what I do for work? And if you are BIPOC the questions that come to mind are even more layered: Will I be the only Black person there? Are these the kind of people that will touch my hair without permission?

The questions can often feel endless.

THE CALL FROM INSIDE OF YOURSELF

Our modern-day disconnection calls for contemporary communal solutions. Luckily for us, the key to solving our collective plight resides within the spirit of those who feel called to gather with others, like you. Heeding an internal longing to be a part of something bigger than oneself can appear in varied ways. There are those who seek to join something that already exists and those who are inclined to architect those very spaces. I would argue that if you are reading this book, it is safe to assume that you resonate with the latter, so my primary goal is to help you connect with how you can do just that. We need you to be activated with your vision and to spread your light, because no matter how similar or unique your idea might be to others, there will always be something special about the way that *you* want to and will do things.

Realizing that you want to architect opportunities for others (and of course you, too!) to connect is enlightening. It immediately ushers in a sense of purpose and expansiveness because the possibilities of what might transpire or be ignited by your efforts are boundless; you truly never know who you will meet or what relationships will form as a result of your vision. Your special way of curating an experience might lead to new friendships, romantic possibilities, business partnerships, and everything else in between. It is one of the many ways that life opens up and shows off just how kismet and aligned our stories can be. As the person curating these moments, I believe that the most important element to consider at the onset is ensuring that your intentions are authentic and good natured.

As the leader of a collective of any kind, your most important responsibility is to ensure that the people you invite into the space you are architecting feel safe and are unmistakingly clear about what they are getting themselves into. You can accomplish part of this through how you describe the community in copy and marketing, but that is just the tip of the iceberg. I believe that the most important factor folks consciously or unconsciously assess is the energy and overall vibe of the person steering the ship. The captain, aka the leader or founder of any group, sets the tone for their community. The way they carry themselves, what they prioritize, their explicit intentions, and how they make others feel in their presence is the ultimate indicator for the trajectory, success, or failure of a collective.

These days we hear a lot of talk about the rise of cult-personality types stepping into leadership roles (in the United States, particularly, we do not have to look too far to see proof of it). Interestingly enough, these personalities are not found just on the world stage or on reality shows, they can also be found among everyday folks, preying on the deepest yearnings of people in vulnerable positions. Some time ago, Twitter/X (I'll still call it Twitter) exploded after a video went viral of a "women's empowerment coach" belittling and humiliating one of her clients during a retreat, in front of the other attendees. To be completely honest, I could not bring myself to watch the whole thing because it was too triggering. Thousands of people on Twitter rightfully criticized the leader (who, by the way, allegedly charged everyone $10,000 to attend this *empowerment* retreat) and highlighted how toxic the situation was, but, for me, the immediate feeling was not anger, but sadness. In this scenario, an adult woman sought community and wanted to be encouraged by someone she has been made to believe "has it together" and can "put her on." This woman started in a position of deference toward the leader because of her perceived idea that there are important things to be learned, which would not be a weakness in the presence of a grounded leader who has taken on the role of teacher. But if the captain steering the ship turns out to just be an insecure Queen Bee on a power trip, this reverence will just fuel their ego. What makes matters even more complicated is that these days such leaders commonly build their influence online, which, as we already touched on in the previous chapter, can often make it more difficult to see beyond the veil of deceit or ulterior motives.

My experience building Goddess Council (GC) taught me countless lessons, but one of the most important ones was the in-real-time reminder that in choosing to bring together strangers I not only had to account for the magic and light they brought into our space, but also their personal baggage and previous experiences that often caused tension both within themselves and with others. Because of this I cannot emphasize enough the importance of intention. As a leader, depending on your intention, you can either help folks become more trusting, vulnerable, and open to community, or you can create an environment that exacerbates issues already present, thus leaving folks worse off than when they met you. This of course does *not* mean that intention alone can spare others from being harmed (sigh, . . . I learned this the hard way) because no single person can ever control the behaviors of others, but at least the foundation an organization is built on can be set with the proper bricks and mortar to ensure the building does not crumble.

As someone who is intrigued and impassioned by the idea of bringing people together with a specific intention, I've found it is important to check in with yourself before you formally create anything or invite anyone anywhere. I implore this because the truth is, humans are unpredictable, and our shadow selves can be tricky with their methods of influence. Some examples of how this can play out in real life include:

- Convincing yourself that you are embarking on something with the explicit intention of helping others, but your unspoken incentive is to be validated by your peers.
- Convincing yourself that you are doing something good for others, but in reality, your desire is to create a space that serves as an escape from elements of your personal life you want to avoid.
- Convincing yourself that you are gathering people together because you like to connect folks, but actually you feel lonely and yearn for friends.
- Convincing yourself that you deeply care about a cause and want to raise awareness, but you are really trying to build rapport with a specific person or company that will lead to your dream job.
- Convincing yourself that you want to be the change and build community around it, but you just want to amass a large TikTok or Instagram audience to get noticed by brands and make money.

At first glance, none of this seems unethical or inherently harmful, but I would argue that the damage lies in the concealed nature of the true purpose. The most important underlying fact of all these scenarios is that it involves people outside of self, and when you involve others, it is imperative to take into account that it's not just about you anymore. When you choose to involve others, you can undoubtedly make a positive impact in their lives, but let's keep it real, this also means that you have the potential to cause harm. As a leader, it is your responsibility to mitigate that risk by being honest with yourself as to why you wish to embark on the quest of building community and what that means. Are you doing this to help others? Or do you want to amass some kind of influence or power as a way to stroke your ego? Do you have the patience to navigate different personalities and needs without centering yourself? Is this truly something that excites you, or something you feel obligated to do?

THE TRUTH HURTS

I am going to admit something I am not so proud of, but it can serve as a learning moment for you, so it is worth admitting. I lost sight of my why, and that was the nexus of why the community I loved so much did not survive. It took me some time to finally admit this, and when I did, the floodgate of tears opened. When I had to let go of GC I could not see past the confluence of factors that were mostly spearheaded by people and circumstances outside of myself. I was beyond disappointed; I was angry, exhausted, and resentful. As the months passed and time created enough distance for me to contemplate and perform a full autopsy of what led to GC's collapse, I realized it was me. That truth broke me, but it was also exactly that . . . the truth and I could not run away from it. When I created GC as a potluck series in my little Flatbush apartment, my why was to bring people together and to feel like I belonged within a space I had the influence to build. Over time, what ended up happening instead was that it became a community for everyone else and I was just the person who led it.

My why slowly morphed into priorities like:

- Taking suggestions from members and obsessing over making them a reality so they would be happy and renew their memberships.
- Ensuring we had enough money in our business account to continue paying the team and covering any business-related costs.

- Brainstorming potential collaborations with brands that would help amplify our mission.
- Obsessively applying for grants and contests in hopes of securing more funding.
- Consistently pitching and finding ways to lock in press opportunities.

Do you see how none of those priorities had to do with me feeling like I belonged? Can you see how easy it was to drift away from the very essence of why this idea came to exist? In retrospect, this arose because I did not intend on making GC a business when I birthed the idea. It morphed into a business because it seemed like the only feasible way to sustain it at the time, and I eventually got caught up in the pressures that came with managing a business. This phenomenon is not just found in my story, it is a theme throughout many career paths and well-intentioned roles. Folks go down a particular path with the full intention of making the world a better place or satisfying a deep yearning to make an impact, only to find themselves with a title that technically aligns with their goals, but is far removed from the expression of influence they imagined possible. It is a theme among folks who work in nonprofits, NGOs, social impact teams, and within the wellness industry. In other words, this is a pattern that appears time and time again among well-meaning leaders. With all of this said, you have to safeguard yourself against this drift and check in with yourself often. Only you will ever truly know the reason why you choose to pursue the path of community building. That comes with the responsibility of staying the course and adjusting whenever necessary to prevent yourself from deviating from your why, your purpose, and a verbalization of some form of your soul's yearning.

I do my best to avoid going down the rabbit hole of what could have been had I paid more attention to the ways I was straying from what I longed for as I built GC, but some days it is hard not to. I built something that helped hundreds of women feel better about their lives, and I helped open up the opportunity for some people to meet their best friends. I wish that magical place of possibilities still existed because it was unlike anything else. It was a space where we could radically imagine, heal, and process all together; but you know what they say about seasons and reasons, right? My journey taught me lots of lessons and only played out in this way for limited seasons. Hopefully, by reading this book you will learn from my oversights and build something that will exist long term. If for whatever reason that does not happen, try to make new mistakes because there is nothing wrong with attempting to create something fresh and realizing it does not work; nothing compares to knowing that at least you tried. Many people do not ever get that far.

Most importantly, do not forget that you are part of the equation. Try your best to avoid neglecting the core of what mobilizes you. Remaining tethered to your truth and ethos is the fuel that will keep you inspired.

REFLECTION QUESTIONS

1. What is your "why"?
2. What is your soul trying to express? How would building community around this expand connection?
3. Is what you are doing right now in alignment with your why? If not, what can you shift today and beyond to help you get back on track?

4. Is this endeavor (or community if you have already built it) still something that feels good to be pouring your sacred life force and energy into?
5. Is there anything about what you are doing that feels like it was externally forced upon you? Do you actually want to be doing this, or are you just afraid of saying no?
6. Are you consistently self-sacrificing to ensure this endeavor (or community if you have already built it) survives? If so, how did you arrive here? How can you pivot to a more sustainable approach?

CHAPTER FOUR
Culture

When thinking about building culture within a community, there are limitless possibilities. It ultimately becomes an exercise of how grand and expansive you're willing to go because this vision can be cultivated into anything you want. In considering this, a quote from *Emergent Strategy: Changing Shape, Changing Worlds* by adrienne maree brown comes to mind:

In movement work, I have been facilitating groups to shift from a culture of strategic planning to one of strategic intentions—what are our intentions, informed by our vision? What do we need to be and do to bring our vision to pass? How do we bring those intentions to life throughout every change, in every aspect of our work?

This often results in groups centering work that doesn't depend on factors outside of their control (such as funders, or elections, which come and go and should be well used but not directive or debilitating). The clearer you are as a group about where you're going, the more you can relax into collaborative innovation around how to get there. You can relax into decentralization, and you want to.[1]

And so, as you embark on a path of architecting a community born from your imagination, consider that this is an opportunity to be radical. There are no limits to how much change, love, and expansion can come from the collective you are attracting to one another. As we expanded on in the previous chapter, the most integral element to consider as the person (or persons) making this community come to life is your intention.

We will explore culture in this chapter by diving into three sections: depth, design, and sustainability. I want to preface this by letting you know that I have been *deeply* inspired by the practices and perspectives of adrienne maree brown and Octavia Butler, so get ready to see their names a lot. To me, these two visionaries not only embody the essence of communal care but also embrace a lens of futurism and radical imagination that has come to influence my perspective about what it means to be someone who is contributing in a positive way to society at large. The commitment to bring people together is not just about intentionality and embracing the most loving elements of humanity, but it is also quite literally a means of survival. In the aftermath of 2020—what I call "the year that changed everything"—I see this more clearly than ever. It is also worth explicitly pointing out that I, as are the femmes who have most influenced my views on this work, am an Afro-descendant. Therefore, the filter I view everything through will always look out for and prioritize the safety of Black people first and foremost. I am too intimately aware of what it feels like to be an afterthought in a space, and any guidance I impart will always encompass elements that ensure fewer people experience that feeling. If you intend to build a community inclusive of all kinds of people, the kind of space that inherently annihilates hate and division, I implore you to train your mind to do the same.

DEPTH

If you are like most people, a part of you craves deep connection with those around you, but you have not quite figured out how to initiate it or where to go to find it. (Might I dare assume that is part of the reason you are inclined to build a community of your own?) This was ultimately the loudest and most obvious feeling that pushed me to build Goddess Council (GC). It was not until I was on the brink of closing down the community that I stumbled upon the quote in *Emergent Strategy* that forever changed me and the way I construct safe spaces: "We need each other. I love the idea of shifting from 'mile wide inch deep' movements to 'inch wide mile deep' movements that schism the existing paradigm."[2]

In a society that prioritizes practically everything through macro influences, the idea of shortening our reach and dilating our depth is subversive. Imagine a life where all your connections and decisions were based on substance and intentionality: your food grown by farmers whose life story you knew well, the sweater on your back created by a designer who you knew prioritized ethical practices, the coffee you drank cultivated by roasters you were proud to know, and so on. I know that these days it's impossible to be tapped into every detail of what we eat or where we shop, but there is one element of how we engage with the world that *is* in our control: how we choose to connect with people. For example, you know how most of us are conditioned to engage in this mediocre exchange:

"How are you?"

"I'm good, you?"

"Good!"

Well, imagine that instead as a collective we began engaging with one another something like this instead:

"Hi, how are you? How's your spirit feeling today?"

"Honestly, I'm not feeling the best. I would rather be on my way to visit my best friend who is having a hard time right now. It isn't easy to focus because I just want to go and hug them and make sure they're okay. Thanks for asking."

"I'm sorry to hear that. Is there anything I can do to help you feel even the slightest bit better?"

This is just a fictional scenario, but do you sense how different that feels? Well, that feeling of care, genuine interest, and being seen is the depth that could serve as the cornerstone of your community if you weave it into the foundation of your culture. In the next chapter we'll dive into techniques you can adopt to actually help people to feel comfortable enough to share openly about how they're feeling, but for now I want to focus on driving home the importance of cultivating an environment that is unlike the one that's typically offered by our hyper-capitalistic / hyper-individualistic society. In other words, the more unique and full of depth and feeling your community is in comparison to the general social constructs offered by the larger world around us, the more tender, expressive, and human those within it will feel safe to be.

In a post-COVID reality, where capitalism and marketing have never ceased their impositions, there's *a lot* of talk about community being the next trend. On TikTok, marketing analysts and trend forecasters are buzzing about how consumers are now interested in feeling a sense of community when engaging with brands, and now companies are scrambling to figure out how to "build community" for the sake of revenue, market visibility, and metrics. To me, this points to a massive issue. Not an issue that we'll have to confront eventually, or something in the distant future, I mean, right now! I can't help but wonder, *Damn, after the insanity we just collectively experienced and survived, the grand shift that society took away from it was that companies needed to "build community" in order to withstand the market?* It enrages me that despite all the proof we undoubtedly have now about the critical role of *true* community, we are *not* talking about how we need to shift policies, government spending, and the demanding expectations of the workplace to prioritize the support of people and how they can sustainably show up for themselves and others. As much as I'd hoped that, coming out of the pandemic, there would be a grand effort to create and fund organizations dedicated to supporting the elderly, unhoused folks, and those in need of access to mental health resources; or, that there would be an expansion of support to women and children experiencing domestic violence given the alarming spike of domestic violence cases reported during the pandemic;[3] what I see taking off instead are corporations creating the illusion of care and tethering themselves to the concept of community.

This is why you, a person who feels called to bring people together, have to remember that it's imperative you prioritize encouraging connections with *depth.* This is what we're both lacking and yearning for within our society. Real people are suffering from the consequences of loneliness and isolation often with no clear path on how to change that. And the cues they're getting from society is that they can access community if they buy certain products or align themselves with brands. I'd argue that those people, and society at large, deserve better than that. They deserve to know what it's like to connect in ways that are anti-capitalist and humanizing.

To me it is obvious that the answers and solutions for building a more vivacious world, full of people who feel seen and supported, lie within you. You would not have this desire to bridge connections and relationships if there wasn't a part of you that (a) desires those very things; (b) knows there's a gap within a certain community that is being neglected; (c) recognizes that you have the skills, knowledge, and passion to do something about it. As you reckon with how you define depth and ways to relay it, approach it all from the heart, because that's ultimately the energy you want to impact within others. In order to evoke a feeling of support and belonging, and make a true impact, whatever you create must be born of and sustained from the heart, not the mind. It doesn't take much digging to notice the blatant neglect people feel within their hearts, and that void without a doubt infiltrates you and creates ailments in a myriad of ways that affect how humans connect with one another. In the United States, mass shootings are a common occurrence, hate crimes are rising as white supremacy weaves itself further into mainstream culture against marginalized groups, bullying is leading children to complete suicide, and so much more. When the state of the world comes up in conversations with friends and family, we just say "the world has gone mad," and as much as I would like to, I can't disagree. It's true. The lack of love is slowly chipping away at some of the most basic tenets of what it has meant to be a principled member of society.

With that in mind, if you are unsure of how to ascertain whether you are making decisions that align with your heart center, close your eyes and scan your body for answers. Ask yourself, *When I think about this idea being out in the world, do I feel a sense of peace or do I feel angst?* This might seem too simplistic of an approach for some, but it is my go-to method whenever I feel dubious about literally anything. There are few things in life I am certain about, and one of them is the fact that our bodies will always tell us the truth. It is undeniable. If you feel peace upon asking yourself this question, take it as an undeniable sign that you are tapping into something that makes your spirit happy. Continue feeding whatever it is you have taken interest in creating because it is generating those feelings of self-gratification and contentment that so many of us chase but don't exactly know where to find. We just have to go out and live, and the feelings will present themselves and let us know that we have tapped into something special. Conversely, if you sense any angst when contemplating whether you should move forward with your idea, consider it a clear indication that you should immediately pause and reassess. This doesn't necessarily mean that you cannot move forward with your vision, but something about the way you're framing it doesn't feel sustainable or reassuring. That angst can mean so many different things, but ultimately only you can decipher it and take the appropriate steps to assuage yourself.

DESIGN

When considering how you want to design your community the most important thing to remember is that no idea or vision is too big. So long as the mission, intention, and depth of the community is set on a solid foundation, you can architect anything.

With that in mind, start off by asking yourself the following questions to stimulate a vision of how you want to bring your idea to life:

- Where will your community gather?
    - Digital only (global)

- **Pros:** You can impact more people, overhead costs stay lower, and some pieces of the experience can remain timeless (e.g., you can record workshops and offer the recordings to people who couldn't attend).
- **Cons:** This encourages more screen time, which is something a lot of people already struggle with; in-person spontaneity won't be possible.
- IRL only (location specific)
    - **Pros:** You can share meals together, hug, and experience city-specific perks.
    - **Cons:** You will miss out on being accessible to people who don't live nearby.
- Hybrid (digital and IRL)
    - **Pros:** You get the best of both worlds and can incorporate the most positive aspects of online and in-person connection.
    - **Cons:** If organized in tandem, more effort will be required to maintain both fronts (this isn't necessarily a bad thing, but it's something that would have to be accounted for).
- Who will be able to access it?
    - Public facing
        - **Pros:** You can cast a wider net and be accessible to more people.
        - **Cons:** There is no vetting process, so you won't have many details about the kind of person you'll come in contact with prior to meeting, which opens up more opportunities for misaligned interactions to occur.
    - Private, application required

- **Pros:** If someone has to go out of their way to apply to be a part of your community, then you have proof that they have read through whatever you've outlined in your application about the community tenets, and they are still in alignment with what you're creating. This preliminary criteria at the onset draws in your ideal community members and organically filters out those who are not interested in what you're creating.
- **Cons:** The process of reading through the responses to the applications can become time consuming.
- Word of mouth only (friend of a friend system)
  - **Pros:** You will create an organic and self-sustaining system of attracting like-minded people into your community.
  - **Cons:** This isn't a fool-proof system as you'll be placing trust in the discernment of others and they might have a differing perspective when it comes to vetting prospective members.

These questions can become even more logistical as you consider:
- How often will the collective convene?
  - Weekly
  - Biweekly
  - Monthly
  - Quarterly
  - Bi-annually
- How will everyone remain in communication?
  - Newsletters
  - Subscription-based message board

- WhatsApp group
- Instagram flyers/posts
- Eventbrite posts
- How many people do you envision at each gathering?
  - Fewer than five
  - Five to fifteen
  - More than fifteen
  - More than twenty-five
  - More than fifty
  - More than a hundred
- Will this community require membership dues or will it be free?
  - We'll explore this further in the following chapter.
- Do you feel comfortable leading events?
  - Do you want to be the main point of contact?
  - Would you prefer to work with someone who is a natural extrovert and wouldn't get overwhelmed by engaging with lots of different energies? (Btw, it's perfectly normal to be someone who can ideate and bring an idea to life, while simultaneously not wanting to be the face of it or wanting to be so visible.)

The list of questions can go on and on, but the more you tailor it to the needs of your specific vision, the clearer it'll become! Personally, if I were to design a brand-new community now I would prioritize in-person gatherings, once per month, with no more than fifteen people; would strictly communicate through newsletters; and would rely on word of mouth as the main way to attract new members.

SUSTAINABILITY

When considering all the possibilities of how your community can exist, it is important to lean into any visionary energy you might be feeling, but it is also critical to be realistic. In other words, you have to be honest about your bandwidth and the inherent sustainability of managing your community. I never considered this when I was building Goddess Council, and it without a doubt played a role in the overwhelm and confusion that ultimately led me to close it down. The intention behind me creating this guide is to hopefully make you aware of all of the things that got in the way of my ability to sustain the community of my dreams, so please listen when I say *do not bypass this part of the process.* Oftentimes when we're excited we just want to do the thing and deal with the problems or consequences as they come, but in this case, that will eventually prove itself to be negligent. Once you open the door to engage with others and make an idea public, things get complicated, so as the architect of this community you have to be clear about as many details as possible at its inception. Of course, other ideas will take form and your vision will expand over time, but as we've already covered, setting down the foundation of your community with precision and mindfulness is *key.*

In pondering how to set both your community and yourself up for long-lasting success consider the following questions:

- Will you like the structure of the community long term?
    - Communities change shape over time and at the onset you can't really account for all of the tweaks that will be made along the way, but you should prioritize maintaining personal preferences that encourage long-term sustainability.

- Does your vision for the community account for the actual amount of labor required?
    - Think about how many *actual* hours you will be required to pour into this every single day, week, and month.
        - I would encourage you to add on a few hours more than expected, to account for any mishaps that will inevitably pop up.
        - If things become more intricate than originally anticipated, prioritize securing help from others so you don't wear yourself out (like I did).
- How many people do you want involved in the maintenance of the community?
    - Will you hire help?
    - Will the community be encouraged to volunteer assistance with any operational tasks?
- How long can you picture being able to manage this community?
    - Is this something you can show up to all year long or would you prefer to embark on this seasonally?
- Do you want to lead this forever? Do you want to enter this endeavor alone or as a group? Do you want to eventually pass this on so you can focus on building other things?

I would argue that this is not only the most important part of the process of building community but also the most fun! There is of course a lot to consider, but this part of your journey as a community architect will feel the most expansive and liberated. These are the elements of this work that will open space for you to connect with the vastness of the possibilities that exist not only around you but also within you.

It's worth noting that although you may be the person who conceived the idea for a specific type of community venture, you do not have to go through the process of creating it on your own. As you know, I established Goddess Council on my own, but ultimately, the assistance of others became essential. At first, I struggled with asking for and receiving help, but I now know that it had a lot to do with my own pattern of hyper-independence. Throughout my journey, I've come to acknowledge that regularly choosing to go at things alone is the antithesis of togetherness. Initiating something on your own could be very helpful, but sustaining it alone is a recipe for disaster—we just are not wired to do things that way. This isn't a point of view I've always had, but it is one I had no choice but to adopt after accepting that I was responsible for making so many areas of my life more complicated than they needed to be by avoiding assistance. I encourage you to discuss your ideas with others in your network. Often it is an excellent way to learn about helpful tools, connect with potential advisors or mentors, and advance what you're thinking about bringing into the world in general. If there aren't people that you can talk to in person, use the internet to your advantage! Create a Reddit thread with questions that others can chime in on, or send a thoughtful email or DM to some thought leaders you look up to the most, asking pointed questions you'd like their perspective on. You never know, they might respond! As you share openly about what you want to launch into the world, you'll get glimpses of how your idea would be received by others in its current state. It can also become an organic way of inspiring and enlightening those who would want to play an official role in leadership. You may enter a conversation with the curiosity to investigate how someone else might interpret your concept, and instead gain a cofounder or other type of organizational leader.

It was during the ideation stage of building Goddess Council that something within me woke up. I realized that I didn't have to be a passenger in society but instead could be one of the people who made it make a bit more sense. In a 1994 interview with the Silicon Valley Historical Association, Steve Jobs had this to say about how we can all show up to life:

> *The minute that you understand that you can poke life and actually something will ... pop out the other side, that you can change it, you can mold it. That's maybe the most important thing. It's to shake off this erroneous notion that life is there and you're just gonna live in it, versus embrace it, change it, improve it, make your mark upon it.*[4]

So, beloved community architect, I implore you to go out and mold this world. On behalf of society, I want to remind you that we need your ideas, we need your light, we need your intuitive guidance. Too many people are growing tired of seeing and feeling that we are neglecting our collective needs. I think in some ways we're expecting a grand shift to just happen one day, but what we fail to remember is that *we* are the change we're waiting for. You are who you have been waiting for, so if you're being called to step up and mold this world into a better version of itself, do not ignore the call. You're equipped. Go out and shake shit up!

REFLECTION QUESTIONS

1. Consider the kind of culture you want to cultivate within your community. Describe the feeling(s) you want to encourage in others.
2. Have you ever entered an experience that was promoting tenets of togetherness, only to find out it wasn't cultivated

to be that? Describe what about that experience space didn't align with your expectations. How can you mitigate replicating those oversights within your own community?
3. What observations have you made about modern-day society that emphasize the cultural impact of current hyper-individualistic attitudes? How do you believe that impacts our ability to experience unity?

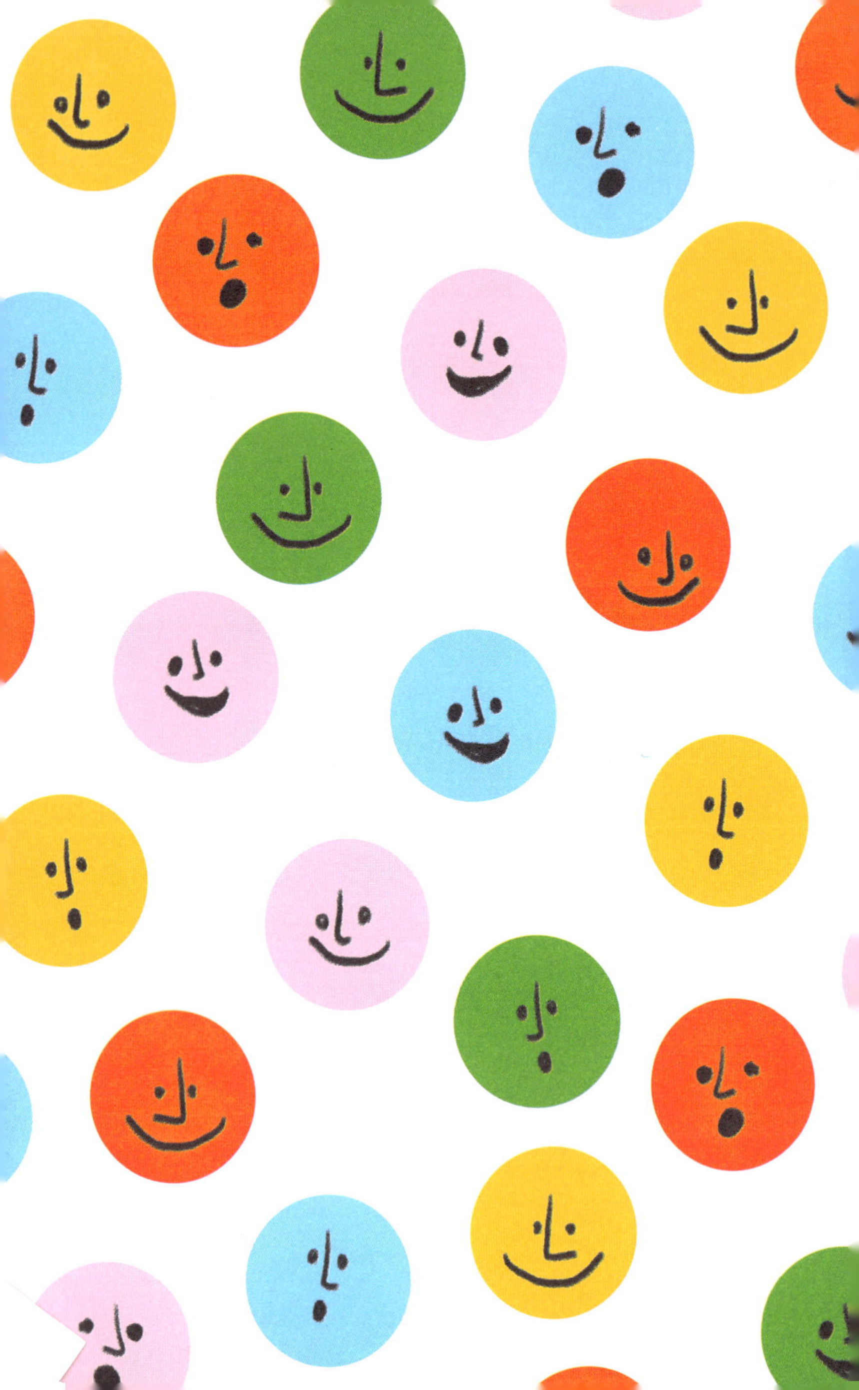

PART TWO
Sustainability

CHAPTER FIVE
Disarming/Safety 75

CHAPTER SIX
Leadership 87

CHAPTER SEVEN
Money 97

CHAPTER EIGHT
Burnout 111

CHAPTER FIVE

Disarming/Safety

Making people feel comfortable in any space that you lead doesn't usually stem from any grand gestures, instead it occurs in the micro-moments: in the small details done without fuss or outward acknowledgment, where you make someone feel especially cared for and considered. Priya Parker, author of *The Art of Gathering: How We Meet and Why It Matters* explores this very theme saying, "Gatherings crackle and flourish when real thought goes into them, when (often invisible) structure is baked into them, and when a host has the curiosity, willingness, and generosity of spirit to try."[1] As a community architect one of the most important elements of your role is to consistently stay a few steps ahead in anticipating the needs of the different kinds of people you could be attracting into any of your spaces. Throughout this chapter we'll explore what some of those scenarios could look like, while unpacking the importance of setting a code of ethics, using contracts to hold people accountable for their role in upholding the ethos of the community, and examining how the facilitator of a gathering is responsible for influencing and protecting the experience.

HOW TO MAKE PEOPLE FEEL WELCOME

When choosing to embark on the fulfilling, yet delicate journey of architecting community, it is imperative to keep in mind the fact that not everyone is exactly like you. While interests and ways of being may overlap (otherwise the community wouldn't exist), every person you attract into your space comes with their own story, life experiences, and oftentimes, baggage. With this in mind, embrace the process of considering the obvious dynamics that could potentially come into play within a certain group, namely race, religion, and culture. For example, as a Black woman, when I see other Black women, I immediately feel more at ease. On the contrary, if I am the only Black woman in a space, I keep my guard up because I am hypervigilant of potential microaggressions and othering. A white person leading a gathering, or simply attending, does not know how I'm feeling, but they can still do something to alleviate that pressure by simply understanding the fact that it is a *very* real experience (this sentiment can often generally apply to any group of people who make up the minority in any group setting, especially when their culture, religion, or race have been stereotyped by larger society in a disparaging way). This could play out in immeasurable ways when considering how the dynamics of religion and culture may also lead others to feel hypervigilant and worried when entering a gathering. So, if you want to appeal to different kinds of people, make sure you use inclusive language to describe your community. This process starts before anyone enters the room. Cultivate this care and detail during the ideation stage. In other words, if it's an afterthought, it is already too late.

    That women's coworking space that I frequented a while back, the Wing, was touted as a third space that would transform the third wave feminist movement by creating a sort of utopia, safe for all women. Needless to say, I was *bought in*. This space included a room for women to freshen up in, offering skincare products, perfume, brushes, and hair tools. Unfortunately, the moment Black women began exploring the room we immediately knew something was off; none of the haircare products catered to curly or afro-textured hair. So, in practice, we were not *really* able to freshen up like the women who had "normal" hair. This is an example of how different kinds of people were not considered during the ideation stage. If this were a space for *all* women then why didn't that consideration go into every detail? Why weren't different kinds of women consulted along the way to ensure that diverse angles were covered? Eventually, after enough Black women mentioned this, curly and coily friendly products and tools were added, but it was all an afterthought. Had this small detail been integrated from the onset, Black women would have gone into the experience without pressure to educate, and therefore would actually have felt safe in that environment. Instead, this need to be vocal about having the right to have the same experience curated for us, as it was for other women, chipped away at that trust. Since the Wing was only accessible via membership, Black women were essentially paying to be in a space that they had to work to make inclusive. Do you see how although the intention of the space and community at large was meant to give *all* women the opportunity to opt into a safe haven, it wasn't actually that in practice? Despite the verbiage the Wing used to articulate its mission and purpose, the actual experience of those words was not the same for everyone.

As a community architect (particularly if you are a white person), you must hold yourself accountable to take caution and consider the ways in which something you build might have blind spots. Here are some ways you can do that:

- Consider how different people may experience your space by asking a diverse group what they would need to feel comfortable in a new community led by someone like you.
  - If your network is not diverse, reach out to people online and set up some time to chat (and intentionally try to make new friends from different walks of life). If you can, pay people for their time, especially if they are women of color, or at the very least make it worth their time to open up and share such helpful perspectives.
- Do your research and learn from others by reading books and listening to podcasts (some of my favorites are recommended at the end of this book).
  - This creates an opportunity where you can learn from already existing information without having to ask anyone to do any labor.
- Learn from the leaders of communities that did not work out. Allow the oversights of others to be an opportunity for you to tune up your perspectives and avoid repeating the same mistakes.

Within the obvious variations of differences previously described, there's another element to be considered: people have different personalities. As the person building a community you have to decide what kind of behaviors and personalities would thrive in the environment you're creating, so let's explore how to account for that.

CODE OF ETHICS

When I built Goddess Council (GC), I did not initially set forth a code of ethics for the community at large. I naively thought it was obvious what we were about and everyone would engage with one another the way I would. In retrospect, this was one of the costliest oversights I had as a leader because assuming anything is never a good idea. Now I know that it is my responsibility within any dynamic to make things clear; even the tiniest of details have to be verbalized, especially when you're bringing together strangers. Throughout the first few years of GC, when we were just gathering in groups of ten or fewer in my apartment, I would add the following disclaimer to every email I sent out the day before our gatherings.

"Hi _____,

I'm thrilled that you'll be in attendance at tomorrow's Goddess Council gathering! Below are some helpful things to keep in mind in order to enhance your experience:

- *We'll officially begin the event ~7:15, so feel free to grab snacks and mingle while everyone trickles in (if you're coming in alone, don't worry, I'll make sure to introduce you to everyone who is already there).*
- *This is a phone-free zone, so please refrain from recording or scrolling once we begin.*
    - *Once the gathering officially concludes, we'll take a group photo and then I'll encourage everyone to exchange info so you can stay in touch.*
- *Do not ask anyone what they do for work. This gathering is an opportunity to connect deeply with other women based on who they are, not what they do or who they know. Instead, ask questions like*
    - *What are you passionate about? What are some of your favorite spots to explore in the city during the weekend? What books or podcasts have you tapped into lately that changed your life in some way?*

> - *What is shared during the gathering stays in the gathering. Nothing that is shared throughout our time together should be repeated outside of the gathering to anyone who wasn't initially present.*
>
> *Here's tomorrow's address (this is my personal home address, so do not pass this along to anyone without my prior approval, thank you!) [ADDRESS INSERTED HERE]*
>
> *I can't wait to hug you! If you have any questions, don't hesitate to email me or DM on Instagram and I'll get back to ya ASAP.*
>
> *Warmly,*
> *Cat, Founder of Goddess Council*

This was my way of setting ground rules for how the gatherings in my home were going to go. It was simpler to enforce them because there weren't that many people, and of course people are less inclined to break rules when they're in someone's home. Eventually though, this wasn't enough, particularly once we shifted into a virtual community in 2020, so, I switched it up and clarified exactly who we were and who would align best with the GC community based on our principles. The code of ethics lived on the home page of our membership website, which we prompted anyone interested in joining us to read prior to entering our virtual community.

> ### Who We Are
>
> *Goddess Council is a wellness community and sisterhood curating intimate gatherings virtually and IRL where* all *women can come together to* engage in soul-centered connections, feel joy, and access opportunities to honor the inner goddess within!

Disarming/Safety

Who Should Join

You should consider joining Goddess Council if:

- *Quarantine has inspired you to seek and be a part of a soul-aligned community*
- *You're looking to be a part of a judgment-free space that will embrace you through the challenges that come along with womanhood and the ups and downs of being a human*
- *You're a WOC looking for an inclusive community that prioritizes your peace, safety, and wellness*
- *You crave a toxic-free community*
  - *No gossip*
  - *No racism, xenophobia, hate*
  - *No cattiness*
  - *No cliques*
  - *No bullshit*
- *You're starting off on your spiritual journey and want access to like-minded women who understand living and thinking beyond the superficial*
- *You're seeking opportunities to evolve into the highest version of yourself*
- *You can honor every woman's goddess-like energy and are looking to connect and cultivate from a heart-centered place*
- *You live in a new place and are seeking to connect with like-minded women locally*
- *You are manifesting a new community that will embrace you with sisterhood energy and will remain invested in your long-term well-being*
- *You're looking to add new fulfilling and enriching experiences into your life*

Although this was simply worded, it helped to set the tone for new members during onboarding and was a great way to create an ever-present reminder available for all members to refer to at any time. It made it impossible for anyone to say they didn't know what we stood for and what we were about. Once members joined the actual community, they were prompted to sign a simple contract that was drafted up by our lawyer, which outlined behaviors that would lead to the termination of their membership.

Some of the ones that stood out included:

- Using GC as an opportunity to brazenly promote their business or harass members to engage in their services
- Any form of bullying or intentionally inflicting harm to other members
- Sharing any private information shared within gatherings to people outside of the community without previously receiving consent

I believe it is an absolute *must* to write out a code of ethics for your community *before* you launch. This will set the standard for how folks experience whatever environment you are building. When crafting your own code of ethics, consider the following questions:

- How do you want people to feel in the spaces you architect?
- If you had it your way, how would everyone interact with one another in your community?
- What would you never want someone to experience within the community you build?
- What is acceptable behavior? What is not acceptable behavior?

As you continue to gain clarity, I would also encourage you to articulate, for yourself as the community architect, the microdetails of the person you believe would thrive (both metaphorically and literally) in the space that you're creating. Within your code of ethics, you can express to others what your community represents and what doesn't fall within the scope of its acceptable behaviors or beliefs. It will also help you clarify the messaging you'll put out into the world to be taken in by others, who can perceive it to either be for them or not. Some of these questions can look like:

- Does this community cater to extroverts?
- Would introverts have a place to retreat to and recharge in between exchanges? Will there be sensitivity around not forcing shy folks to speak aloud unless they are ready?
- Will our gatherings be loud and party-like or lowkey?
- Will there be booze? Will there be mocktail options?
- Will we encourage drinking alcohol of any kind?
- Are we smoker friendly? Cigarettes? Weed?
- Is open dialogue around religion and/or politics allowed?
- Is it okay for people to solicit within the space? If so, what are the boundaries?

I want to underscore that the goal should be to create an unwavering level of exactness when it comes to thinking about the ways you want to encourage people to commune. This makes it easier to precisely communicate and attract your target audience, which will more easily bring forth members of your community once you exit the ideation phase. Over time, some of the things you thought would matter to you don't, or maybe details that you hadn't considered during the ideation process will present themselves. Either way, it's important to communicate the code of conduct you expect everyone to abide by, update it accordingly, and inform community members of any changes as they come up—preferably in writing. This can be as formal or informal as you deem necessary for the needs of what you are envisioning, but it should be something that can be shared and accessed at any point by anyone it pertains to.

CONTRACTS

I know now that the most helpful way to uphold the code of ethics you draft for your community is to have all members sign a contract agreeing to the terms upon sign up. This is one of the details I learned a little too late while building my own community. I naively believed that because of the way I spoke about GC and how I carried myself as the leader of the community, everyone involved would immediately understand what it stood for. And, for three years while our community met exclusively in-person, there were no misunderstandings or complications (at least not that I'm aware of). This track record led me to believe that everyone was on the same page; however, once we shifted into a virtual model that's ecosystem was built exclusively online, the level of miscommunication and boundary crossing increased. Unfortunately, because of this, people got hurt. Since I had no contract everyone had to sign upon joining the community, I never had a clear outline of the consequences of certain behaviors. This made it difficult to prove to those who were hurt that clear action would be taken. At the same time, I was unable to clearly prove to the person who violated the code of ethics that their behavior was out of line.

Ultimately, the best approach to take when it comes to making the inner workings of your community feel as legitimate as they are, is to take every step possible to ensure that nobody is unclear about anything. A contract does not have to be an overly complicated legal document full of intimidating jargon. It can be simple. It can be whatever you want it to be; just make sure that it outlines the expected terms and the ramifications of violating them. As the community architect, sit with yourself and contemplate the ways you intend to protect your community's mission and code of ethics. Here are some questions to help clarify your thoughts:

- What are the non-negotiables that will immediately have someone removed from the community?
- If someone violates a specific rule outlined, how can you go about mediating?
- How much or how little information should anyone share with members of the community if there is ever an investigation into someone's actions?
- Will you create a board that will review any intermember concerns? Is this something you will handle directly?
- Will there be a way for members to safely report any perceived violations without it being made public to all?

As often as you can, create opportunities for yourself to imagine potential scenarios that could appear within your community and among the people you intend to attract. Anticipate the potentialities and create rules and solutions around them so that you're not caught off guard if they ever come to fruition. As you'll learn, there is no possible way to get ahead of every single thing that might happen, so don't get too carried away with trying to account for an unlimited amount of possibilities. Just know that as time goes on and you learn more, your contracts can be updated and folks can choose to recommit.

As a community architect, it is your responsibility to do your best to create an environment where as little harm as possible can come to be, and enforcing contracts is one way to do that. As Priya Parker describes in *The Art of Gathering,* "In a group, if everybody thinks about the other person's needs, everyone's needs are actually fulfilled in the end. But if you only think about yourself, you are breaking that contract."[2]

With all of this said, please remember that humans are fickle and complicated, so there could very well be instances where despite your best efforts, something goes wrong. Know that so long as love, compassion, and an intent to understand remain at the forefront of your actions, you always have the capacity to find solutions. Will everyone always agree with your solutions? No. But, ultimately, you are the one who designed the community, and with proper counsel and/or strategies you will make the best possible decision to protect members.

REFLECTION QUESTIONS

1. Contemplate and outline the subtle (or not so subtle) considerations that make you feel more welcome in an environment. How can you integrate those details into the settings you are seeking to create?
2. Reflect on the ways you can explicitly express your commitment to creating a safe space for those who align with your community mission and happen to be a part of an underrepresented group(s).

CHAPTER SIX

Leadership

The way in which a community is managed and who leads its ethical, moral, and logistical direction are critical to its very existence. I am going to be up front with you by saying, as the leader of Goddess Council (GC), I did not know what the hell I was doing. As you now know, I basically stumbled into architecting this (epic, unforgettable, one of a kind) community, so I was making critical foundational decisions while leading based on intuition, not necessarily strategy. Now, do I think I was a bad leader? No. Could I have done a better job if I had already possessed certain skill sets and had a support system? Absolutely. Realistically speaking, all leaders have room to improve. There is a never-ending amount of information about people, society, and how to actually connect and love that should be integrated into leadership practices. In a perfect world, global leadership would be heart centered and embody the kind of guiding energy that ushers folks into a reality where the best elements of human creativity, collaboration, and connectedness can thrive, where those ensuring that the community thrives have a deep vested interest in trying to make it function smoothly.

When I started GC I did not have a truly informed opinion about what it meant to be a good leader, but, the woman now writing this guide has five years of grassroots/high-stakes/

self-directed experience, and I want to share it all with you. For many months after closing down GC I convinced myself that I must have been a bad leader, otherwise, my community would still be up and running. Now that I can view my past self with a more compassionate lens, I realize that by choosing to cease community operation and acknowledging that I was not fit to keep it running, I made the best decision for myself and everyone in the community. I heeded the warnings and knew when it was time to throw in the towel, despite being advised to do the opposite. My goal throughout this chapter is to share all of the things I learned while I tried to rise to the occasion of evolving into a community leader, as a mostly anxious twenty-something with barely any experience but with a lot of heart. Throughout my experience as a founder/CEO/facilitator with Goddess Council I was on what now feels like a five-year unpaid internship that changed my life. I did not exactly know what rules and ways of operating would suit me or the community best; I had never brought strangers together, led vulnerable group conversations, or managed a business where I had to pay taxes! I did not have a mentor or friends who were doing anything similar, so oftentimes I implemented strategies that seemed like great ideas but were uncommon. In retrospect, this is something I love about my journey. Since my imagination was not bogged down by the rigidity of rules, I had no foreseeable bounds. Everything seemed possible. That's what made Goddess Council so special: we were all learning as we went along. As a result, our community members saw their insights and suggestions implemented quickly. But they also witnessed leadership failures in real time. There are so many layers and themes to unpack about all of this. Let's dive into it all, shall we?

FACILITATOR

The facilitator of any given gathering sets the tone for the experience that everyone will have. There are both subtle and overt ways in which this plays out, and all elements are necessary. The facilitator must connect with the purpose of a gathering, understand the nuance of personalities at play, and maintain a harmonious balance, all in real time. A great facilitator knows that they hold the power to steer the experience in whatever direction they deem fit but uses soft power to enforce it. I would describe soft power as an unspoken energy embodied through action and assuredness. A great facilitator makes direct eye contact, can ease concerns, gently redirects conversations when they begin to stray, and most importantly, can encourage depth and connection without being forceful. Okay, so, you're probably wondering how do I get there? What do I need to do? On one hand, I enthusiastically believe that many of these skills can be learned and built upon. On the other, I believe the following key character traits and skills need to be present first:

- Need to have a high emotional quotient (EQ).[1] Without emotional intelligence and the ability to effectively lean on healthy interpersonal skills and emotional regulation, a facilitator cannot inherently make the space they're cultivating for others feel smooth enough to become expansive.
- Cannot run away from being the focal point of attention. In other words, a leader has to be comfortable enough with being perceived by a group as a center that this pressure does not lead to shutting down or becoming so distracted by anxiety that they cannot do their job.

- Narcissistic tendencies are completely at odds with this role. Being able to consistently reroute attention to others and avoid consistently centering self is critical.
- Need an ability to listen to others for extended periods of time without feeling the need to unnecessarily interject.

One of the coolest factors about facilitation is that it does not actually begin when everyone is together, but long before that. As we have explored in previous chapters, understanding the ethos of the community and therefore being able to clearly outline dos and don'ts is imperative to upholding an experience that all consent to. With that said, I would encourage these guidelines to be communicated in writing prior to any specific event or gathering. This will begin to set the tone for a collective experience long before it actually takes place. In addition, this also makes everyone aware of which behaviors will and will not be encouraged, and for many this will immediately create a sense of safety. For example, if you give a clear warning that the use of any and all racist or homophobic language will lead to the person being asked to leave the event and being removed from access to the community, most POC or queer folks will take that disclaimer at face value and feel somewhat assured that they'll be safe and protected by leadership. If done right, a facilitator can open the space and serve as the conduit to a pathway for conversations and connections to go deeper. Ensuring at the onset that everyone is on the same page about the goal of the gathering and how respect can be extended to those participating before entering a room together is one of the simplest and most effective forms of communication one can incorporate as a leader and facilitator.

Once folks come together in a room, the facilitator's presence should remain clear and direct, while maintaining a certain level of distance that encourages free-flowing exchanges and "aha moments" between those present. In other words, this is where the practice of active listening and "connecting the dots" come together. The facilitator is responsible for actively circulating the energy of a group and directing it toward depth, togetherness, and expansion. Essentially, it is the delicate art of tying together themes within the unique perspective and shares of those present to highlight the cohesive and overlapping nature of the collective's experience, without stating the obvious. In cultivating the experience's energy this way, folks will slowly begin feeling deeper within themselves and seeing those around them with a layer of closeness and familiarity, making it easier to share openly. This interactive leadership role does not entail just filling up space by being the center of attention. I would argue that it is actually quite the opposite. Yes, the facilitator should have an obvious presence so that those gathered are clear on who is leading, but never to the extent where it seems like the facilitator is the star of the show. Within GC, I took on this role often; these are some of the ways I made it less about me and more about we:

- Introducing folks to one another early in the gathering to begin cultivating familiarity between those attending.
- Using names when addressing folks, so that others can have a higher chance of remembering them.
- Forming in a circle or arrangement where folks are sharing out loud, encouraging folks to face each other.
- Saying reinforcing phrases like "Thank you for sharing" or "That was beautifully said," especially after someone has shared something vulnerable.

In general, the facilitator of any gathering has to remain keenly aware of their responsibility, because it is not a passive role. If you choose to facilitate any kind of gathering, my hope is that you want those in attendance to have an unforgettable experience where they can sincerely explore both themselves and others. Please be intentional and take this role seriously and understand that your presence (or lack thereof) can make or break an experience.

BOUNDARIES

Depending on the nature of your community, boundaries will look different. For example, if your community exists solely online, there are things that you won't have to consider that you would in an in-person community. The ground rules and code of ethics you outline to serve as the foundation of how the collective operates will uphold and reinforce boundaries, and personal boundaries typically stem from there. A community needs boundaries that are upheld by leadership and boundaries within leadership, but members will also naturally come up with boundaries. Ultimately, the most important thing a leader can do is to create an environment where all boundaries are respected and their expression is encouraged.

Individual members enter the community with their own narratives and previous experiences, so unpacking the reasoning behind why they are the way they are is not as important as simply honoring where they are and avoiding the exacerbation of trauma. Specific boundaries set forth individually can typically be accommodated, but if there comes a time where someone's boundary goes against the flow of how things operate, it is within leadership's discretion to pause and make a decision about any misalignment. I remember a member telling me that they did not like receiving email communication and preferred texts, but email was the primary way I shared information with the community, so I offered this: they could either receive the emails or miss out on the information that would grant them the opportunities to be an active community member.

In full transparency, when actively building communities that attract people who are strangers, you will notice just how intricate people can be. Some folks are inherently more agreeable than others, but you will likely get asked to accomodate in ways that you would have never thought of on your own. To that I say, that is the nature of this all. The more you get to know folks, the more obvious it becomes that we are all *really* different. As a leader of any group, it is critical that you remember this. When the time inevitably comes where you feel caught off guard by someone's request or complaint, try to take your own ego out of it and pay attention to what they are trying to communicate. This does not necessarily mean that whatever they ask will be accommodated (because sometimes people really do the most and you have no choice but to put your foot down), but it is always worth creating a dynamic where people feel safe enough to express their needs to you.

Sometimes boundaries must be set within and for the community management team (or the group of people leading an organization at any given moment) as a way to protect the sanctity of the mission. In the early days of GC, I had to do just this. At the time, we had no budget to pay folks to serve on the team, so I relied on myself and whoever volunteered assistance. There came a time when someone new had moved to the city and enjoyed a gathering they attended in my apartment so much that they felt inspired to ask to assist me with running things on the back end. They seemed nice and outwardly embodied everything that GC stood for, so I immediately said yes and began onboarding them to facilitate some gatherings. We talked for hours about the future role they would play in the organization and it became clear that if we had a budget, they would be getting paid to help run the business.

Eventually, I realized that while this person did enjoy the essence of everything GC stood for and was making new friends, they were also interested in using it as an avenue to meet new romantic partners. When it dawned on me that they had an ulterior motive, I became uneasy because having this person serve as a facilitator and part of the community management team already somewhat skewed the power dynamic (since they were responsible for moving around the energy of our gatherings and making people feel comfortable). There was a risk that things could go really badly within the romantic dynamic they initiated with members, and that it could impact how members related to the community. I mean, if someone you had a fling with upset you and you did not want to see them again, would you ever show up to an event they were leading? No! So, as the leader of the community I had to decide whether this was an element that I was okay with being baked into the foundation of GC, and the answer was . . . no. At all costs, I wanted to ensure that members who turned to GC as their home away from home, would not have to deal with the possibility of their personal lives encroaching on how they were treated as members (there was also the potential for preferential treatment or for having private information shared within the team to trickle down to a member).

Ultimately, I encouraged the volunteer to either stick to just being a member and reaping the benefits of experiencing the community without access to all of the BTS (which from

Leadership

my vantage point was a great option, given that all they would have to do is show up and have fun) or to remain in leadership with the understanding that they would need to tread carefully when it came to seeking out romantic connection with members because of the skewed power dynamic. Despite my working with my therapist to prepare for this conversation and writing out notes on how best to communicate all of this, the person did not take well to my pointedness. They interpreted it as a personal attack. They claimed that everything I said was rooted in an archaic perspective of power dynamics, and they went as far as to claim that I was perpetuating heteronormativity by getting in the way of queer romance. Now . . . as a person recovering from a deep tendency to people please and avoid rocking the boat at all times, this was just one of those moments where I could see that if I did not lean into courage and protect the essence of the community I had worked so hard to design, it would unravel or be tainted later on. It was difficult to have someone so deeply misunderstand my intentions and label me as someone I was not, but I knew I could not stray away from what I felt was necessary. Protecting the community and the dynamics that took so long to form was my primary goal.

This experience played a massive role in my ability to honor myself and my ideas enough to set forth a clear delineation of what was working and what was not. Making people happy and creating copacetic environments makes me happy, but being a leader means sometimes having to make tough decisions or be unpopular. When you can perceive potential threats to the calmness of the collective, it is your duty to ensure that the risk is mitigated. If not you, then who?

REFLECTION QUESTIONS

1. Contemplate on how you can enhance your EQ. What training tools and resources are available to help you expand the skills you're looking to advance?
2. What personal boundaries do you find helpful in your interpersonal relationships? How would these boundaries translate in the group dynamics of your future community?

CHAPTER SEVEN

Money

Having the idea to architect a community is wonderful. As we have already explored, too many people are lonely and isolated in a society that is abundant with resources and opportunities that should be extended outward, for the collective's advancement. Since don't see this play out on a macro level via institutions and systems, everyday people must offer solutions. In other words, anyone who feels called to fill the gap should without a doubt embark on that journey because the world is starved of community. Let's get real though . . . nothing in this life is free and money is a factor. When I first started hosting the Goddess Council (GC) potlucks I tried to ignore money and was just completely enamored with the idea of hosting badass women in my home and filling them up with food and booze. It was not long before I realized that I was the one subsidizing it all and . . . I was *broke.* Although my immediate thought upon embarking on the journey of building GC did not relate at all to money, it became impossible to ignore that none of it would come to life without some kind of financial investment. I do not know about your financial position or how much wiggle room you have in your budget to cover the costs of gatherings, but like I said I *was broke* and could not afford to continue hosting potlucks on a biweekly/monthly basis without charging it to my credit card and choosing to pay it off slowly. Something had to give.

Throughout this chapter we will explore the approaches I used to subsidize GC gatherings at first, and how the financial aspect of running the business eventually took form. I want to make it clear that I would not necessarily consider myself to be financially savvy, do not have any ties to investors, and have never had financial backing from anyone to fund my ideas. With that said, if you are in a different financial position than I was, some of the tips and approaches shared in this chapter might not apply to you. If that is the case, at the very least, exploring these options will equip you with resources and solutions that you could pass along to someone else! Looking back on my journey now, so many moments of clarity and reprieve came from talking to people in my network about how stumped I felt in this arena. Since I do not come from money nor has anyone in my immediate family operated a business in the United States, I had no font of information that could trickle down to me and make this journey easier. I depended heavily on the network of women entrepreneurs I was building along the way to show me the hacks and illuminate the possibilities I didn't know were available to someone like me. My hope is that if you find yourself in the same position I was in, this chapter will offer you information that will allow you to hack the money element to community building so that you can focus on putting your vision into action and impacting lives.

The ideal scenario when architecting a community and bringing people together is to simply focus on cultivating the human experience. But, under capitalism, things do not quite work like that (lol) and whether we like it or not, money always has to be a consideration. Things cost money; unfortunately that is just the way it is. So, for a collective to take form in a free yet practical way requires a method of operating that relies on some form of subsidies and/or volunteers. When I consider this concept, what comes to mind is potluck-style gatherings, where everyone takes on some level of responsibility and all elements of putting together a gathering are checked off without too much falling on the shoulders of a select few. Also, the structure of parent teacher associations (PTAs) comes to mind because the system works as such: within schools, parents or guardians take on roles without being compensated, but work together within a collective to advance a mission (in this case, making kids happier, healthier, and better supported academically). There are different ways in which communities can be structured. They can be as casual or official as the founder envisions, but regardless, money will remain a factor. From the vantage point of trying to create an ecosystem where money can be funneled into your community, without having to pay it back or fall into debt, I suggest you consider these four avenues: grants, bartering, partnerships, and crowdfunding. While there will always have to be an exchange of time and labor by the community organizers that keep everything together, these four routes will ensure that money does not become an obstacle. Let's explore the these options and how they played out in my experience!

GRANTS/CONTESTS

To put it in layman's terms, grants are kind of like contests. You do not know if you will receive an award, but it is always worth applying for. The worst-case scenario is that you do not receive the money; the best case is that you are gifted money that you do not have to pay back, which you can use exclusively to do great things that will allow you to make shit happen! In my experience, the announcements of grant opportunities have exclusively come through word of mouth by direct peers and friends, or by coming across the information on Instagram. For a long time, I would see these announcements and keep on scrolling because I had the attitude of *Why would they choose me?* or *So many people are going to apply for this, what's the point of even trying?* But now, having won three grants I can say that I was very wrong. Look, I get it. Taking thirty minutes out of your day to submit long responses to questions for an opportunity that you might not get doesn't seem appealing. It becomes yet another thing to add to the list of things to do during the day, and quite frankly it is one of the few optional tasks in adulthood we can opt out of, but ... isn't the possibility of winning free money worth it? Additionally, there is an advantage that you have in these situations that isn't so easy to gauge in the moment, but ... most people will not actually apply. The pool of applicants usually is not as big as you imagine because the majority of folks have that *What is the point of applying?* mentality. So, if you are one of those people who actually put time and effort into your responses, paired with the attitude of *Why not me?* you will be surprised at the possibilities that open up for you.

Throughout my journey in this, it dawned on me that there are real people reading these applications, so if your story and responses are appealing, you will be considered. It truly is as easy as that! One detail in my experience that I would be remiss to not mention is that every single contest or grant application I applied for that was directly sent to me by a friend, I received. In other words, when your community sees an open opportunity in the universe and immediately thinks you and your idea would be perfect for it, run with it! The first time it happened to me I thought it was just good luck, but after it happened again and again I realized something else was going on. My woo-woo side tells me these things kept happening because each time these opportunities were sent my way I received them wrapped in the hope, love, and belief of my people. Them believing it was a possibility in and of itself opened up space for me to believe that it was something worth throwing my name into the hat for. Life has taught me that sometimes others can really easily see your potential and/or the potential of your ideas, even when you may not connect easily with it yourself. I believe that nudges from the universe can flow through those around you. In other words, if someone says "I saw this opportunity and thought of you" take it as a sign!

Switching to a logistical note, I found it helpful to create a document where I stored all my written responses to grant/contest applications. Oftentimes, you will find an overlap in the questions typically asked on applications. So, if you store your responses in a document, you can just refer to and repurpose them every time you submit an application. This will make the process less daunting over time, while also cutting down the time it takes to complete the process! *Think smarter, not harder boo!*

BARTERING

Bartering is one of the oldest and most universal economic systems. It explicitly requires community support and collaboration because when exchanging resources and/or skills, no money is involved. When I first started GC, bartering was the primary currency exchange I could offer. From website design to social media management, all of it was navigated without actual cash, but with the support of people who believed in GC's mission and were directly benefiting from the spaces I was architecting. The people who helped make GC "a thing" behind the scenes never had to buy tickets to gatherings, got free merch, and were always credited for their role in helping us succeed. Personally, bartering has impacted my trajectory as a creative for close to a decade. When I started out with blogging or with my podcast, I would agree to write and publish interviews so long as the person I wrote about confirmed that they would share the post on their own platforms as a way to garner traction for my work. In terms of Goddess Council, one example that stands out is when I reached out to a skincare company and asked if they would be open to gifting products for a giveaway to our membership community in exchange for promotion on our private platform. If this is something you are interested in exploring, please don't hesitate! So many people are willing to get creative about ways to collaborate with others, you just have to be clear on what you are asking for and what you can offer. You should do this reflection before attempting to initiate a conversation with a potential partner so that the terms are clear and they can have access to all relevant details in order to make a decision about whether they want to participate. Otherwise, you run the risk of appearing disorganized or unreliable at the start—especially if this is the first time you initiate a conversation with a new person or group.

As you consider what you'd like to propose and who you want to collaborate with, it's important to ensure that what you are asking for and what you can offer are comparable. If your ask of the other person is hefty, what you give in return should be as well. Every case is specific and has its own details, and that makes it difficult to offer you a foolproof formula that would apply to every single case. I would, however, encourage you to be practical and put yourself in the position of your potential bartering partner. If you were in their position and presented with the opportunity you have in mind, would you agree to it? If a part of you thinks that something about the exchange feels inequitable then it's safe to assume that whoever you present it to would feel the same and you should reimagine your proposition. When taking into account what a fair bartering trade can look like, keep in mind that what you can offer may not be what the other party needs. In other words, don't view things as being worthy of exchange only if they are exactly proportionate. The goals of the other party may be completely different from yours, so learn what they are lacking and offer to use your resources to help them acquire what they need. In a world where everything costs money, bartering can often seem a less valuable way to exchange with others, but I would argue that there is more nuance to the equation than first meets the eye. Often, money is the main factor that holds folks back from making their ideas come true. In that, too many great people and paradigm shifting possibilities are unfortunately lost. Bartering creates space for those very people, and their collaborators, to avoid the blockages that come with being able to access capital thus advancing their ideas and limitless possibilities.

    Radical thinkers often embrace the concept of bartering as a way to ensure that nobody is left out of society because they do not have wealth. Part of the beauty in community is seeing everyone as valuable members of the collective who will always have something they can contribute to make the lives of others better. It has always been a pain point for me that bartering isn't a system that manifests more in Western societies. Maybe that is a direct result of capitalism's grasp on how we believe we are destined to operate, but maybe it is because most of us are simply not in community with others as much as we used to be, so who exactly would we barter with? Maybe it is a blend of both. Regardless, I am here to remind you that this is always an option! It will require you to think a bit out of the box and propose skill or material exchanges that most folks do not immediately consider, but that does not make it any less effective. Get clear on what you can do for others either via the community you're cultivating or in other ways and allow that to be your guide. Without a doubt, you have something to offer that would be a great benefit to others. Do not be shy about your gifts and instead use them to your advantage by bartering with people around you (or on the internet!) to create solutions for whatever problems you are trying to solve!

PARTNERSHIPS

When I think of partnerships, I imagine a merging of an experience or idea that benefits everyone equally. These days, most partnerships manifest on social media via giveaways, mentions, takeovers, and so on. While those options are helpful, I would like to encourage more depth and consideration. When considering a partnership that aligns with the advancement of your community, consider things holistically. You can start off by asking yourself these questions:

- Does this brand or company align with our community ethos?
- Does the leadership of our potential partner embody the ethics of the community?
- Is our community solely being used to help with the "image" of the potential partner? If so, does that feel good?
- Do the partnership terms feel equitable? Is the community, brand, or leadership going to be exploited in any way?

In the past, whenever I agreed to partnerships for GC, I always had to consider how the experience would leave me feeling. I poured so much love into cultivating an experience within our community, which felt wholesome and safe, so I simply did not consider any opportunities or people who came along that I did not feel would align. Beyond that, my filter for good partners was not necessarily the same one that most folks would look for. While metrics and algorithms are important aspects to consider when trying to attract more community members online, it is *not* the most important heuristic to consider. Instead, think about the depth of the experience that will emerge via the partnership. In doing so, you will have to consider the *number* of people who will be impacted, but more importantly you will have to consider *how* they will be left feeling. What will the lived experience be as a result of this partnership? Will it make people feel something meaningful? Will there be some kind of long-lasting positive impact by whatever emerges from what is created? These questions are important because truthfully speaking, people are tired of the surface-level nonsense. There is so much nothingness taking up space online and on people's feeds. If you are going to make a buzz about something, make it worthwhile! Make it mean something. If a partnership is underway, look at it through the lens of how it can benefit others versus exclusively considering how it can benefit the brand. I believe this approach is helpful because, if you are creating opportunities that are of service to others, it will organically attract community support and new members. The authentic desire to show up for others via whatever partnerships you pursue should ultimately be the goal. In doing so, you show up for the community and they will in turn show up for you.

CROWDFUNDING

According to Wikipedia, crowdfunding is the practice of funding a project or venture by raising money from a large number of people, typically via the internet. Similarly, fundraising in the context commonly used now entails acquiring financial investments from lenders in exchange for part-ownership of the business. It's important to make a distinction between crowdfunding and fundraising because both are commonly explored options, but vastly different. Crowdfunding can simply be the process of acquiring donations from the public, without having to give them anything in return. It is customary to offer some kind of reward or product in exchange, but it is not compulsory. Whereas the implication of accepting money from an investor is that they expect to be paid back and to receive some kind of long-term additional benefits. I never considered going down the route of seeking formal investors, and instead found alignment in crowdfunding because I didn't enjoy the idea of having to deliver on promises to a lender that I inherently could not guarantee. By way of crowdfunding, Goddess Council gained the opportunity to expand and think bigger, but without the pressure to pay back the investment made by others. Instead, people chose to support us financially because of the impact they already saw us making.

As someone who has invested in the crowdfunding campaigns of others and successfully organized one myself, I can confirm that this is a great option to raise money, it will just require a lot of effort to bring to life. As with all options proposed in this chapter, opting to pursue this route to secure resources will depend extensively on your community. Crowdfunding is an option that highlights the impact of micro contributions, word-of-mouth, and support in all forms. My first successful crowdfunding campaign took place in 2013 when I raised $1000 to equip the underserved kids in my family's neighborhood in Santo Domingo with school supplies to help kick off the start of their school year on a high note. The next prosperous crowdfunding campaign came by way of the IFundWomen of Color initiative. GC had just secured a $1000 grant on their website (I told you it's worth applying!!) and along with it came the opportunity to build out a campaign throughout about five months with the support of the IFundWomen team. Throughout that process it became clear that if I was going to encourage people to extend their financial resources to support the work of GC it had to be worth it. So, I worked with our small team to iron out the details of what our campaign would look like and ultimately shot for the moon, with the confidence that we'd somehow land among the stars. After so many months of preparation we launched our campaign and had exactly four weeks to reach our goal. We started out with a goal of raising $50,000 (told you we shot for the moon lol) but within two weeks realized that it was out of reach for our network and lowered it down to $10,000. Ultimately, on the very last day of the campaign we reached our goal and were elated that we were actually able to do it! Ironically, only a few short weeks later it became clear to me that GC would have to embrace its end.

    Online and in-person, I was questioned about why I would go about putting in so much effort into crowdfunding only to close the community down, as if it was premeditated, but now I can confidently say that this crowdfunding experience was partly to blame for the exhaustion and overall burnout I was forced to confront. In retrospect, I know that if I had more support across the board, the crowdfunding experience would have been more manageable. And, despite the toll it took on me personally, I still stand firm in my position that crowdfunding is a *great* option for communities who need financial support but, like I said, it requires a lot of effort. In the next chapter, we will get more into the burnout element of my journey, but first, here is an honest list of things to keep in mind if you're going to pursue building out a crowdfunding campaign:

- In my experience, it took over fifty hours on the back end to bring the GC campaign to life and about twenty hours of promotion after it went live. Be prepared to invest *a lot* of your free time in a campaign that will hopefully reach its financial goal, but also may not. Pursuing this route requires a balanced amount of optimism and realistic expectations. Approaching this process with total commitment and confidence that it will play out perfectly, while also being mentally and emotionally prepared if things don't work out as you hoped, is essential. If your crowdfunding bid fails it does not mean your idea is not worth pursuing; it's okay to be disappointed, but don't take it as an absolute sign of defeat. Find assurance in the fact that you are putting effort toward trying to find solutions and that something will work out, one way or another. This is also why it's important to remain open-minded and curious about trying out different funding methods, possibly at the same time. It keeps your options open and lessens the risks of having all of your eggs in one basket.
- Your marketing strategy *will* require you to directly ask people for money. If you have a difficult time asking for help, this process will make your ego squirm with angst, but you'll have to do it. There is no other way to go about it if you're serious about pursuing every possible opportunity to reach your goal.

- You have to be okay with becoming the person who you sometimes get annoyed by online when they post multiple times a day to promote their business. On average, someone will have to come across your campaign seven times before actually contributing, so increasing visibility in the promotion phase is critical.
- You will have to be meticulous with how you design your campaign landing page. To entice potential donors to actually explore your campaign and not exit after a few seconds, make it interactive, colorful, educational yet concise, and, simply put, pretty to look at. This means, you might have to spend a lot of time exploring ways to put together cool graphics (platforms like Canva are perfect for graphic design beginners), hire a visual artist to bring your campaign to life, or barter with creatives in your network to build out the areas you lack skills in.

Regardless of the path you choose, remember that you have options. If one avenue does not work, try another one. Your commitment to making your community thrive should be enough of a driving force to avoid giving up on confronting the inevitable hiccups. You may feel discouraged while trying to build something out of nothing (especially when money is involved), but it's what you do in the aftermath of disillusioned moments that make up the future of possibilities.

REFLECTION QUESTIONS

1. For every category outlined in this chapter, explore some real-life examples that exemplify those specific financial models, and then see if any of the examples resonate as a model you'd like to use as inspiration.

2. Using the categories outlined in this chapter as a guide, consider the extent to which finances have to be considered within the scope of the gatherings you want to create for the community you have in mind. Make an honest assessment of how the idea you have in mind will translate materially, and then clarify the financial model you'll ultimately opt for.

CHAPTER EIGHT

Burnout

The act of bringing people together as a community architect is oftentimes a path filled with purpose and joy. But no matter how much you love doing something, the possibility remains for becoming exhausted and ultimately burned out if you don't put the proper care practices in place. I learned this all the hard way. It is the reason why I had to make the choice to cease operations at Goddess Council (GC). I was not well. The irony of managing a wellness community that supported others while simultaneously withering because of it is not lost on me. That chapter is now far enough behind me where I can reflect on the woman I became when I reached rock bottom, and while I feel saddened for her, I know now that I learned some important lessons during that time. My hope is that you can learn from the me who made the decisions, and ultimately mistakes, that led to burnout and avoid repeating the same patterns as you navigate your journey of service and community building.

BURNOUT DEFINED

The term "burnout" was coined in 1975 by Herbert Freudenberger and defined by three components:

- Emotional exhaustion: the fatigue that comes from caring too much, for too long

- Depersonalization: the depletion of empathy, caring, and compassion
- Decreased sense of accomplishment: an unconquerable sense of futility or feeling that nothing you do makes any difference.

In the aftermath of closing GC and acknowledging that I was in the thick of experiencing burnout for the first time, I picked up the book *Burnout: Completing the Stress Cycle* by Emily Nagoski, PhD, and Amelia Nagoski, DMA, and it was only then that I was able to get clear on what the hell was going in my body, mind, and spirit. I'll refer to these women a lot throughout this chapter because they changed my life and equipped me with the perspectives and language I wish I had long before diving into this work. I believe that part of burnout prevention is understanding what it even is so that you can pick up on the indications of it within your own life and curb problematic patterns sooner than later! What the Nagoski sisters taught me early on in their book that radically shifted my perspective is that I had fallen into the trap of the Human Giver Syndrome (HGS) without knowing it. Amelia defines HGS as the false, contagious belief that women have a moral obligation to be pretty, happy, calm, generous, and attentive to the needs of others. Throughout the book, they highlight that women are generally the individuals that suffer most from HGS because societal gender roles encourage us to lean into the giver role rather than prioritizing ourselves. I realized that this was without a doubt the energy I was unknowingly embodying as I led Goddess Council. Additionally, I came across the term *careaholic,* which Bryan Robinson, PhD, defined as "someone who has a strong need to be needed and uses caring and helping in the same way alcoholics use booze to self-medicate pain or cope with stress."[1] So, I was not only dealing with the consequences of existing within the HGS paradigm, but I had also become addicted to caring for others.

For context, it is worth noting that GC peaked during the pandemic. I was running a wellness community organization during a time when folks collectively needed community support more than ever before; we had no idea what was going to happen to us on the other side of this never-before-seen experience (at least not in our lifetime) and were leaning on each other to make it through each day. My response to the stress of it all was to throw myself into serving others instead of prioritizing my own stability and sanity. At the time, it felt like I was doing the right thing. I was playing my part and pouring light into the world, which felt noble and healthy. Simultaneously, I was depending heavily on wine and weed to help me get through the tough emotional weight I felt on my shoulders, to survive for myself and to continue building a space that so many were leaning on during their periods of isolation. Additionally, I was trying my best to maintain my own personal relationships while taking in the reality of the racial reckoning in the wake of George Floyd's murder. It. Was. A. Lot. As the Nagoski sisters highlight so well in their book, emotional exhaustion leads to burnout. They describe the unraveling by saying

> *Once you have become emotionally exhausted you can struggle with depersonalization. This is when you are struggling to maintain your compassion and empathy for others. Emotional exhaustion is also characterized by a decreased sense of accomplishment. This decreased sense of accomplishment is a feeling that nothing you do matters.*[2]

To really drive the severity of this experience home for you, it's worth sharing that in 2017, a research article in the journal

PLOS One examined the physical, psychological, and occupational consequences of job burnout. The authors reviewed sixty-one prospective studies and found associations between burnout and serious health problems, such as increased alcohol consumption, coronary heart disease, depression, sedentary behavior, obesity, and musculoskeletal pain. BURNOUT IS NO JOKE PEOPLE!!!!! It can manifest physically as well as emotionally. When we're burned out, our amygdala—the brain's danger detection system—might "hijack" our frontal lobes, says Leah Weiss, a mindfulness expert who teaches a course called "Leading with Mindfulness and Compassion" at the Stanford University Graduate School of Business. This can trigger a fight-or-flight response, which makes it difficult to think clearly, draw conclusions, and recall memories. Burnout is also linked to hormonal imbalance, hair loss, changes in menstruation, stomach problems, and sleep disruption, according to Weiss. People suffering burnout commonly report headaches, muscle aches, and listlessness.

As much as I don't believe in fearmongering, this is one topic of conversation that I cannot stress enough. Burning out feels like subsisting off fumes, but once you actually burn out, it feels like your engine no longer works. Do you know how expensive it is to replace an engine? How absolutely devastating it is that you can no longer use your vehicle to get places and live your life? Consider your body as the most important car you will ever take care of and avoid ruining your engine. Take care of yourself and remember that you simply cannot pour from an empty cup. A true community will never promote exhaustion and depletion, instead it will be restorative, patient, and sustainable. Too many community leaders, including myself, fail to remember this. We get so caught up in serving others that we forget we are people too. What makes things even scarier is that oftentimes, the people we're serving become so used to us relating to them in a certain way that they can't even tell we're withering because we don't let them see it. Please use my story as a case study and avoid making the same mistakes I did; take breaks, check in with yourself, ask for help, and prioritize the hell out of your well-being so you can continue bringing people together in whatever way you're destined to.

ALIGNMENT

Okay, since we've explored burnout, it is only fair to talk about the opposite experience: alignment. Alignment is the sweet spot. It is the feeling of being in the right place, doing the right thing, and feeling like the ideal version of yourself. Regardless of what approach to community building you take, the goal is to feel like you're in alignment. You picked up this book because you feel called to be a gatherer, you know there is more depth to be experienced with and among the people around you, and you know that you possess something that you can alchemize from your magical ideas to make people *feel* more. Acknowledging that calling in and of itself is alignment. It's a truth within you, and the continued expression of that truth in a way that is *not* detrimental to your body, mind, or spirit is what it means to embody alignment. There are moments in life where things feel synchronous, and we can look around and confidently feel purpose, pleasure, and perfection. Of course, life isn't always made up of those feelings, but, on the other side of burnout, I can now acknowledge that being attuned to the needs of my soul inherently opens more space for me to feel alignment. For people like us, there's an intrinsic nudge that tells us that we're in alignment when we bring people together in an intentional way. I need you to understand that not everybody sources a feeling of alignment from this role. On the contrary, a lot of folks feel intimidated by community building, if not outright turned off by the idea altogether. I say this because I want to emphasize that this is not only a necessary role that we must honor as social creatures but also a gift. It is a gift to be an alchemist, and to be able to draw out in others one of the best possible feelings on the human spectrum—a sense of belonging.

As we touched upon earlier in this guide, the world is made up of too many lonely people right now and community—*especially community rooted in love*—is the antidote. I say this with all of the sincerity and seriousness possible: The world needs you. We need you to be in alignment and honor the gift of community building. Whatever your idea is, make it happen! Like Priya Parker so beautifully alludes to in her book title, there is an art to gathering people, and while it's not always straightforward or easy, it is always worth it. No matter where we find ourselves on the spectrum of location, race, class, gender, sexuality, political affiliations, whatever. WE NEED PEOPLE! So, please go and make this world better by honoring your own desire to be an aligned beacon of light. You are here, reading this book for a reason, and I want you to know that you have everything that it takes within you to make our world a warmer and more compassionate place for us to coexist. The only way to go through this whole life thing feeling happy and fulfilled is to have others to share it with. Go on, beautiful human, build the communities where people can find their people. We will all be better for it.

REFLECTION QUESTIONS

1. What steps can you take to avoid going down the path of burnout as you architect a new community, or nurture one that already exists? Take into account your habits and patterns as you consider boundaries that you might choose to put in place.
2. Explore real-life examples of people who you see as models of what it means to be in alignment with what they dedicate most of their time to. What about the way they live life stands out to you and exudes the energy that they are doing exactly what they are meant to be doing? How can those people serve as role models for your own life?

CONCLUSION

Wow, and just like that, you have made it to the end of this book. Hopefully, by now you feel equipped and empowered enough to shift your desire to create the community of your dreams into action, and to transform the world by your vision. Individual actions accumulate to become vast shifts so please remain steadfast in knowing that you are the beacon of hope; you hold the light we are all looking for. Modern times make it easy to forget about the power that inner transformation holds, but it is no secret that once we change, the world changes around us. One of the throughlines of this guide was to reassure you that you *can* make a difference in your life first and foremost, and then in the lives of others; it starts with reconstructing your belief in self. The mere intention to bring us closer to one another is the radically imaginative energy that will bring forth a society centered around peace, unity, care, and love. Moreover, acknowledging that pulse within you that knows things can be better is, to me, the essence of faith. It means you are here to architect the new earth that many feel is already upon us, we just need the right leaders to help carve out the paths toward liberation. With that in mind, it is important to remain aware of the fact that you may very likely have a vision that is ahead of its time, and you may not receive some kind of grand acknowledgment of your efforts or immediate signal of approval from the universe, but as long as you remain grounded in your mission, the extra is just that . . . extra. Ultimately, you know when you feel aligned and at peace, so as long as you remain connected to your unshakeable inner compass,

Conclusion

that is all that matters. The confidence that stems from moving to acknowledge the inner, and knowing that you are capable of reconstructing the world around you, can never be quantified or fully recognized by anything or anyone outside of you. Only you reside in your body. Only you occupy your mind. Only you know your inner truth.

In my twentyish years of being actively online from the days of MySpace, AIM, BBM, Live Journal, and Tumblr, to now Twitter/X, TikTok, Threads, and Instagram I have observed a growing conflation between having a large audience and fostering connection/tangible societal impact, which convinces many of us that unless we have massive social media platforms or work on behalf of an influential company or organization we will not and cannot be taken seriously. Society seems skewed to prioritize and reward efforts that reach hundreds of thousands or millions of people, while glossing over the efforts taking place at the micro level. It feels like an insidious aura that when confronted always brings about a daunting feeling within me because if that helpless feeling is multiplied by an entire population, then I can see a reality where folks avoid even trying to do anything, despite their soul tugging at them to alchemize their gifts.

This is the exact energy I was confronted with when I first began speaking with agents to publish this book. The universe ultimately connected me with a publisher, Parea Books, that has made this process a dream, for which I am forever grateful, but at first, I was told hurtful things that acutely poked at the anxieties I already carried about my ability to create an impact. Primarily, that I was not popular enough for people to take me seriously, and that I was not qualified to have an opinion about architecting community since I technically failed when

Conclusion

I chose to close Goddess Council. Being told these things at a time where a deep sense of confidence was still molding inside of me threw me off kilter. At some level, I wondered if maybe this was just the truth and that sooner or later I was going to have to come to terms with some heartbreaking certainties. I ruminated over the possibility that some ideas never come to pass because they are simply not meant to be and that is just part of the human experience, but a small flame inside me provided enough fiery passion to burn down any thoughts that attempted to thwart this goal. I conceived the idea for this book for a reason, and I was going to find a way for it to be born through me. Similarly, once you connect with the idea for the community you are being called to architect, and the mission behind why, you too will come to feel that sense of unwavering assuredness. One way or another you are going to manifest the community you dream to be a part of because deep down you cannot deny that you are eager to experience environments that allow you to be seen for who you really are, and to act upon the values you cherish most alongside others.

It cannot be denied that having a large platform means that more eyes and ears can be reached, but just because a person or organization can wield influence for collective change does not guarantee that they actually will. As I write this, I hear many people voicing feelings of disappointment at celebrities and artists they have long held deep admiration for because, despite the massive reach their appeal to peace would have, they are either choosing to stay silent in the midst of an active genocide or, even worse, pretend as if nothing is happening. The idolization many people once had for these strangers they formed parasocial relationships with is now shifting to deep appreciation for the courageous leaders who have proven their commitment to being for the people. Many are realizing that they have been existing under an illusion of mutual care by those they have revered and would rather put their support behind people they can be in a reciprocal community with. Most of us know that there is a deeper layer to humanity and collectivism that we are not connected to, and as a result, we are seeing fragmentation across so many areas of life, but it does not have to continue that way. As we have learned time and time again, the solutions to our problems will not magically appear from institutions or government. We have to take individual actions that amass to collective function and successively initiate the rise of new systems that serve us all. We are the ones we are looking for.

As I mentioned at the beginning of this guide, this book is my Trojan horse. I wrote it as a way to equip you with details about how to initiate architecting an intentional community; however, my covert objective stems from a more vulnerable plea: You are needed. We need every person who is here to spread love and inspire unity to lean in and start making things happen. Every day we see new indications of callousness toward one another that were not previously present. This phenomenon paired with the planet struggling to manage so much mistreatment is pushing too many to the brink of desperation, and while I know that we alone cannot solve every source of agony in others, we can stand together as we try to make it through. I hope you do not interpret that as something to be overwhelmed by because truthfully, the way in which you are needed does not require you to be anyone other than who you are really meant to be. The only work required is for you to recognize the calling within yourself and act. If you avoid allowing doubt to consume your mind and grant people permission to reflect that you can be taken seriously, you position yourself to become the change Octavia Butler always talks about. The ways in which you wish things were different can be adjusted and you are perfectly equipped to initiate the updates required. This does not mean you have to find yourself speaking on stages or amassing a million followers online. Bringing together even two people who are in alignment with the mission of your community is already a pretty big deal. I can write this with certainty because I was once so overwhelmed by the state of the world that I would consistently spiral into panic attacks, but eventually something switched within me and allowed me to transmute that debilitating energy into movement. Now, here you are reading a book I wrote and got published without the accreditation of an institution, the backing of an influential company, or monetary wealth. This book is in your hands because I decided to believe that I had the capacity to create the thing I kept searching for. I trusted that if I put action behind doing the thing, I would attract the community that would be in perfect alignment to bring this to life, and that is exactly what happened. I completed this guide while hearing that I was a failure for closing down Goddess Council, recovering from burnout, bouncing back from a divorce, moving to a new country solo, burning through my savings, and witnessing a genocide unfold on my phone. Yes, I am proud of myself for this, but I am only sharing it to highlight that I too have struggled with doubts about whether I have what it takes to make some kind of change on this increasingly chaotic planet. I too have felt alone in my desire to be a part of a thoroughly transformed world. I too have been seeking leaders I could be inspired by. In between the feelings of hopelessness, a small flame remained lit within and encouraged me to lean into the

Conclusion

possibilities that have not presented themselves yet. I wrote this book because I wanted to make a difference in the best way I knew how, but along the way I was transformed. This publishing journey has become proof of exactly what I am trying to encourage you to believe is possible. Without this project I am not sure if I could have sustained the belief that perseverance under the most overwhelming circumstances can in fact still lead to beautiful outcomes.

In other words, this book is not just a book, it is a container full of my hopes and dreams that one day we will find our way back to one another, so from the bottom of my heart, thank you in advance for committing to help make that happen.

RECOMMENDED READING

Below is a list of the top books and podcasts that I recommend for any of you who want to continue learning from some of the thought leaders who have impacted me the most. Of course, the learning doesn't end here, but it's a great place to start.

PODCASTS

Finding Our Way hosted by Prentis Hemphill
How to Survive the End of the World hosted by Autumn Brown and adrienne maree brown
Unlocking Us with Brené Brown hosted by Brené Brown

BOOKS

The Art of Gathering by Priya Parker
Braving the Wilderness: The Quest for True Belonging and the Courage to Stand Alone by Brené Brown
Emergent Strategy: Shaping Change, Changing Worlds by adrienne maree brown
How We Show Up: Reclaiming Family, Friendship, and Community by Mia Birdsong
Parable of the Sower by Octavia E. Butler
Take Care of Your Self: The Art and Cultures of Care and Liberation by Sundus Abdul Hadi
Together: The Healing Power of Human Connection in a Sometimes Lonely World by Dr. Vivek Murthy

NOTES

INTRODUCTION

1. Trojan horse: someone or something intended to defeat or subvert from within, usually by deceptive means. Merriam-Webster, https://www.merriam-webster.com/.

CHAPTER ONE: BELONGING

1. Wiktionary: The Free Dictionary, https://en.wiktionary.org/wiki/communitas.
2. Dictionary.com, https://www.dictionary.com/browse/belongingness.
3. *Brené Brown: Create True Belonging and Heal the World*, https://lewishowes.com/podcast/r-brene-brown-create-true-belonging-and-heal-the-world/#:~:text=Bren%C3%A9%20Brown%20has%20a%20lot,the%20opposite%20of%20fitting%20in!.
4. The US Surgeon General's Advisory on the Healing Effects of Social Connection and Community, Our Epidemic of Loneliness and Isolation, https://www.hhs.gov/sites/default/files/surgeon-general-social-connection-advisory.pdf.
5. National Academies of Sciences, Engineering, and Medicine, Social Isolation and Loneliness in Older Adults: Opportunities for the Health Care System, https://nap.nationalacademies.org/catalog/25663/social-isolation-and-loneliness-in-older-adults-opportunities-for-the.
6. Mother Cabrini High School, https://www.wikiwand.com/en/Mother_Cabrini_High_School.
7. "The plug" is a term used to describe someone who is a resource for obtaining something valuable that would otherwise be difficult to obtain. Urban Dictionary, www.urbandictionary.com.

CHAPTER TWO: GODDESS COUNCIL

1. Dori Lewis, Reclaiming Your Magic and Healing the Sister Wound, https://www.reflectivehealing.com/blog/fortcollins/therapy/reflectivehealing/the-sister-wound-and-womens-circles#:~:text=Simply%20put%2C%20the%20sister%20wound,in%20relationships%20with%20other%20women.

CHAPTER FOUR: CULTURE

1. adrienne maree brown, *Emergent Strategy: Shaping Change, Changing Worlds* (Chico, CA: AK Press, 2017), p. 70.
2. brown, *Emergent Strategy*, p. 70.
3. Amanda Taub, "A New Covid-19 Crisis: Domestic Abuse Rises Worldwide," *New York Times*, April 6, 2020, https://www.nytimes.com/2020/04/06/world/coronavirus-domestic-violence.html.
4. Steve Jobs, interview by the Silicon Valley Historical Association, 1994, https://www.youtube.com/watch?v=kYfNvmF0Bqw.

CHAPTER FIVE: DISARMING/SAFETY

1. Priya Parker, *The Art of Gathering: How We Meet and Why It Matters* (New York: Riverhead Books, 2020).
2. Parker, *The Art of Gathering*.

CHAPTER SIX: LEADERSHIP

1. According to Merriam-Webster online, emotional quotient is the ability to recognize, understand, and deal skillfully with one's own emotions and the emotions of others (as by regulating one's emotions or by showing empathy and good judgment in social interactions), https://www.merriam-webster.com/dictionary/emotional%20quotient.

CHAPTER EIGHT: BURNOUT

1. Bryan Robinson, "The Danger in Caring Too Much: 6 Steps to Avoid Compassion Burnout," *Forbes Magazine*, July 11, 2020, https://www.forbes.com/sites/bryanrobinson/2020/07/11/the-danger-in-caring-too-much-6-steps-to-avoid-compassion-burnout/?sh=748cf7ea3515.
2. Emily Nagoski and Amelia Nagoski, *Burnout: Completing the Stress Cycle* (New York: Ballantine Books, 2020).

GODDESS COUNCIL HOST HANDBOOK

In February 2020, I began drafting up this handbook as a way to assist incorporating new hosts in new cities as Goddess Council expanded. It took me about a month to complete, but by the time I did, the 2020 pandemic was in full swing, so I never passed this handbook along to anybody. As I re-read it and thought about whether it should be included in these pages, I couldn't help but realize that this handbook was the initial iteration of this very book! I hope it serves as a tangible reminder that every idea has to start somewhere. I hope it initiates some kind of inspiration and get put to use in whatever way you see fit.

If you're receiving this handbook it's because you're interested in becoming an official Goddess Council host in your city, and wow, I'm so excited that you're stepping into such an important role in your community. The voice you're hearing as you read this is mine, Cat! I'm the founder of Goddess Council and a fellow host currently based in Brooklyn. Let me start off by just saying that never ever *ever* did I imagine GC to take off in this way.

In the beginning of 2018, I started this community out of my very first apartment because I was desperate for friends. I'd moved to Brooklyn at the end of 2017 and found myself six months in without any friends, and I deeply craved a sisterhood. I randomly got struck with inspiration to "manifest" the sisterhood I was looking for and put it all on the internet—the rest is history. What initially started off as four strangers in my apartment blossomed into gatherings that held ten, fifteen, and then forty people. It was then that I realized I wasn't alone in feeling alone. (See what I did there?)

Fast-forward to today and you're reading this handbook and preparing to foster the same magic in your local community. I can't help but reiterate just how important and beautiful this is. We're living during a time where our society is suffering with deep feelings of isolation, loneliness, and rejection. While you may not know it yet, there are lots of people looking for a light they can gravitate toward to heal the feeling of "not fitting in," and you're about to create a space and community they can *finally* belong to.

Ultimately, your role as a host is what leads people to consider Goddess Council as part of their self-care. It is you who make our goddess attendees feel safe and welcome in any space.

You're the one who eases the anxiety of a newcomer.

You're the one who opens the door to new possibilities.

You're the one who bridges connections IRL that will without a doubt change the lives of those at each gathering.

There are basics to hosting, like serving food and drinks, that you'll be expected to do, but the most important elements of being a Goddess Council host can't be seen with the eye. Your role is to make people *feel taken care of, seen, and accepted.*

The world can be isolating and pushes so many to feel lonely, but any space where Goddess Council's energy is cultivated is a safe haven for those looking to get out of the shadows.

Your role is to nurture and usher in a sense of community that people everywhere are desperate for. What an honor, right?

This organization feels like my baby. It means everything to me, and I wake up every day knowing that it's impacting the happiness and awakening the goddess within so many. Now, I pass my dream to on you because GC was never meant to be fostered by me alone—it's for all of us.

I've put together this guide to give you an understanding of what our values are as an organization and to also share the tips I've learned along the way as I've facilitated gatherings for hundreds of goddesses in my home.

I'm grateful you're along for the ride and can't wait to see the remarkable change you create in your community. THANK YOU!

Soulfully,
Cat

AMBIANCE

Here are some ways to set a warm and welcoming ambiance before your gathering begins!

- Cleanse your space
  - Use cleansing herbs like sage or sweetgrass or holy wood like palo santo (sourced ethically of course) to ward off any negative/stagnant energy that may be lingering around. Use this time to instead invite positive energy and thoughts in your space. Be sure to open a window or door for a few minutes after you finish your cleansing ritual to let it all out!
    - This is also a great time to set an intention in your space. Ask yourself questions like,
      - "How do I want the night to go?"
      - "What do I want people to feel when they walk through the door?"
      - "How do I want to show up for everyone tonight?"
- Light candles

- Creating a warm tone throughout the shared space makes a HUGE difference! Remember, lots of people are coming to your place straight from work or using the gathering as a way to relax from their hectic lives. Don't we all love to light candles when we begin to decompress?
- Add flowers or plants to the gathering area
  - Bring some life into your space, literally! Adding fresh-cut flowers or healthy plants around your space infuses vibrance and life to the energy of the room. And it makes everyone really happy.

Consider your home to be a third space, a place in between work and home where attendees can come to learn about themselves and others. Consider the little ways that will make people feel like they *belong,* that will make them feel rejuvenated, taken care of, and supported.

THINGS TO REMEMBER

Throughout the evening, everyone will be looking to you to ensure they have the best experience possible. Of course, the magic of our gatherings stems from the collective energy of those present, but ultimately you set the tone. With that in mind, here are some things you should remember:

- Whatever vibe you set off is the one that will be followed so it's important to ground yourself before engaging the group. Take an hour or more before everyone arrives to relax and clear your mind. Take a warm shower, drink some tea, or do whatever you know feels good to you!
- Gatherings should be kept to max *fifteen people* to ensure the intimacy of the conversation and connection. Along

the way we've learned that any group over twenty is a bit difficult to ensure everyone gets a chance to speak and connect with everyone else.
- Establish *consistency*! If you want your local GC community to truly connect and build deep friendships, *show up*! The more gatherings you host the better! If you go too long without hosting a gathering people will start to feel disengaged and/or forgotten about.
  - Hosting at least one gathering per month is highly encouraged

PRE-GATHERING

An initial call will be set up with you after you've been accepted as an official Goddess Council host! This time will be set aside to assist you with planning your first gathering and will serve as an opportunity to brainstorm ideas, ask questions, and walk through any concerns you may have.

POST-GATHERING

After your very first gathering we'll hop on a call or communicate via email—whatever you prefer—to chat about how the event went. We'll go over improvements that can be made and things that worked out well! Our team will send all attendees a post-gathering survey one to two days after the gathering where they can submit testimonials, share suggestions, and opt to sign up for your city's WhatsApp chat!

HOSTING A GATHERING

Welcome

SETTING THE TONE

It's important to keep in mind that many people coming into the space are shy, timid, or have some general anxiety about "putting themselves out there." Calming down people's worries in subtle ways (through body language, tone of voice) as they enter the gathering makes a HUGE difference! Below are some of the tried and tested hacks for making just about anyone feel comfortable.

- Hugs > handshakes. Handshakes set a tone of formality, which isn't what our gatherings are necessarily going for. Instead, we want guests to feel like they're entering a warm space full of potential friends. If you can go for a hug it's best, but it's obviously important to respect someone's personal space so if they'd rather not, that's okay too.
    - **Tip:** If someone extends their hand for a handshake, saying something lighthearted like "I'm a hugger" could bring their wall down a bit!
- Disarming the first couple of people may feel the most challenging because you will have to spend more one-on-one time with them, but this provides a chance to build a great connection and sets the tone for everyone who arrives afterward. This offers a great one-on-one opportunity to greet them like a friend and have a conversation.
    - **Tip:** Asking questions like the ones below are helpful ice breakers!
        - "How was your day?"
        - "How are you feeling?"
        - "What brought you here today?"

- The goal is to have guests unwind and feel taken care of. Pointing guests to the food or serving them something to drink is one of the simplest ways to make anyone feel at home.
- Introduce people to each other so there isn't any awkward tension. The key is to have guests feel safe and included, so breaking that wall for them is a great way to avoid having anyone standing around alone. As more people start to come in, introduce them to people in the room, walk them over to where they can sit, and try to stay around until the conversation gets going.
- **Goal:** Disconnect people from everything that happened in their day to where they are right now. Help them connect to others and feel at home.

Mingle

NAVIGATING THE GRAY AREA

Allow a thirty- to forty-five–minute window before you kick off the goddess circle, so people can chit chat, eat, and warm up. This is a great time for people to get acquainted with each other and the space. As the host, this is your time to let people know who you are, how your day has been, and to acquaint yourself with the guests. It's also an opportunity to ask guests more pointed questions about who they are or what brought them into the space; this applies to one-on-one interactions or in a subgroup.

Once it is time to get into the actual conversation (typically an hour after the official start time) gently tell everyone to gather around to officially kick off the goddess council circle.

Kick Off the Conversation

OPENING UP THE CIRCLE

As the host and facilitator of the evening, everyone will look to you to keep the flow going. It's ultimately your role to make the conversation feel productive, helpful, safe, and fair. Here are some tips I've learned along the way that I think will help with that!

- Thank everyone for attending. Remind people why they are there, honor them for intentionally being a part of the community, and assure them of the experience you'll be helping to cultivate for them.
    - **Tip:** Here's a sample of what to say to start the circle.

    Thank you, every single one of you, for taking time out of your day to show up for yourself, to replenish your soul with community and connection. It's not easy to do that when we live in big cities, when we get caught up in work, anxieties, and our day-to-day tasks. But this is a healthy part of caring for ourselves. You should be proud of yourselves for acknowledging that community is an important part of our well-being and gifting it to yourself.

- Introduce yourself formally by name and affirm that that you'll be facilitating the conversation, but ultimately, it's a collective experience.
- Before you begin, take a pulse check of the energy in the room. I typically do this by going around the room and asking everyone to say their name and share how they're feeling at the moment.
    - **Tip:** Everyone is entering the space with varying emotions and energy, so being aware of what you'll be navigating is *really* important to know at the onset.

- Kick off the gathering by reminding everyone of the theme! After a brief description of the theme of the gathering and a bit about what inspired it, I usually ask "Is there anything jumping out of anyone that they want to share?" Typically no one has anything to say, but it's a good way to create some pause and open up an opportunity for someone outside of yourself to speak.
- Ask a general question that will serve as an icebreaker. If no one answers, give your own response!
    - **Tip #1:** Before the event reflect on questions you are curious about related to the theme of the evening topic. It's good to have a few questions prepared in the event you have a shy group who isn't jumping out to share or riffing off of each other's ideas. And then typically someone will respond to your response.
    - **Tip #2:** Sometimes there is a pause, but people are processing what you are saying. Don't rush to fill the silence; people will start speaking once they've thought about what they want to share.

Once It Gets Going

FACILITATING THE GROUP CONVERSATION

- The first time people share out loud they will typically share a lot. While this is totally okay, it's important to be aware of guests that take up the space of others. If someone is going on a tangent, gently interrupt, comment on what they said, and then direct that energy to someone else. It's your role to create balance so also be mindful of people who are trying to share but haven't had a chance to and create opportunity for their voices to be heard.

- **Tip:** If someone is trying to share but getting interrupted, you need to advocate for that person. Gently saying "I think [name] is trying to say something" is usually enough of a nudge to get others to quiet down.
- Typically, the gathering won't end at nine (if it's happening during the standard seven to nine p.m. event slot), but I like to do a time check at nine by saying "I just want to be mindful of your time and let you all know that it is nine o'clock. I'm not saying you have to leave right now but in case you do have to leave this is a head's up."

Wrap-Up

FINISHING WHAT YOU STARTED

In my experience, I find it a good stopping point to close the circle by 9:20. As you'll see, people have shared vulnerably and touched on many topics, so mindfully closing out the evening is key. Abruptly ending such a sacred and meaningful experience isn't ideal for anyone. Here are some things I like to do when closing out:

- Thank everyone for coming and for the energy they put into the conversation.
- Encourage people to stay in touch with each other through the WhatsApp group chat, Instagram, or in person outside of GC gatherings.
- Let people know about future events and opportunities to connect again.
- Ask people to share ideas for future gatherings.
- *Just a head's up, people don't immediately leave; they linger around for another twenty to thirty minutes. Usually, everyone is out by ten p.m.*

HOST REIMBURSEMENT / PAYOUT STRUCTURE

We offer a flat payout rate of $50 for *gatherings* if more than 3 tickets are purchased (at a minimum of $25). If more than 5 tickets are bought, the payout will be base rate plus $5 per ticket (e.g., if 15 tickets are purchased, you would receive the $50 [base] + $75 [override per ticket] = $125).

If you facilitate a formal *workshop*, we pay $60 if more than 3 tickets are purchased (at a minimum of $35). If more than 5 tickets are sold, the payout will be base rate plus $7 per ticket (e.g., if 15 tickets are sold you would receive the $60 [base] + $75 [override per ticket] = $165).

You can receive payment via PayPal, Cash App, or Venmo. Your preference of payment type must be clarified prior to hosting your first gathering. Payouts will be submitted within 15 days of a successful gathering.

Reimbursement for food will also be added to the payout at a rate of $4 per person (e.g., 10 tickets sold equals $40 reimbursement). Upon purchasing any food, send a photo of the receipt to hi@goddess-council.com to assure reimbursement. *Without this, we cannot guarantee that you'll receive the full amount spent.*

FOOD SUGGESTIONS

Throughout the gathering people will want to munch on snacks and sip on something yummy, but you won't have to worry about throwin' it down in the kitchen—light bites and water/tea will be enough!

Presentation makes a huge difference in making your guests feel like they're being taken care of and pampered, so go all out and jazz up your food spread. Use cute bowls, serving plates, and cutlery. Any time we get together it's a celebration, so bring out your best! It's up to you on the kind of snacks you want to provide your guests, but it's always recommended that you provide options as people vary in their dietary needs, and who doesn't like choices?!

Food recommendations include:

- Chips paired with guacamole/salsa
- Fruit salad (strawberries and grapes are always a hit!)
- Cookies
- Cheese assortment and crackers
- Assortment of non-caffeinated teas (with the option to use honey or brown sugar)
  - We recommend chamomile, lemon balm, and lavender
- Pastries
- Sparkling water, orange juice, or water
  - Fruit-infused water is always a win!

Serving alcohol during the gathering is not permitted as it takes away from the sacredness of the conversation. We don't know what battles people have in their personal lives, so keeping our sacred spaces free of substances is super important!

If your community wants to have a fun night drinking, we recommend meeting for a night out at a bar or hosting a casual BYOB event, but avoiding heavy topics and vulnerable sharing during the evening. We're all adults and we'd never get in the way of fun or autonomy, so as long as alcohol isn't present during official goddess circles or any formal gatherings it's fair game!

SUBMITTING A GATHERING REQUEST

The creative team will work BTS to manage marketing and circulate information for all events that you'll host. Since there are many moving parts that go into this, it's important that we receive the hosting details of your gathering *at least* four weeks ahead of the projected date. This will give us enough time on the back end to do everything necessary to make sure you receive as many guests as possible!

The guide below outlines the information we'll need from you in order to list your proposed gathering and begin collecting RSVPs:

- Date
- Time
- Event description
- Event type (e.g., workshop, gathering, meet-up at a bar)
- Location

Our team will send you all marketing assets within seven to ten days of receiving the required information along with the link to RSVP so you can promote your gathering online.

IDEAS FOR GATHERING THEMES

We recommend creating diverse options for gathering types! Remember, you're not limited to hosting just one gathering a month—you can have as many as you think fit the needs of your community. Below are some ideas for a diverse set of gatherings that you can easily host at your place!

- Traditional gathering with a set theme and goddess circle
- Movie night
- Potluck brunch
- Sip 'n chill

BOOK CLUB

As a host, you can opt to facilitate a monthly gathering to unpack and discuss a book! Book themes should center around growth, spirituality, and fictional stories with strong feminine leads. Ultimately, the goal is to read books that help everyone become more grounded in their uniqueness, strength, and personal journey.

At the end of each book club chat, choose the next month's book! To make choosing a new book fair, have everyone write a book suggestion on a slip of paper and put it in a bowl. Whichever book is randomly picked out is the one for the next month! We suggest hosting these during early Sunday afternoons.

The fee for book club will be $10. As the host you'll receive 80 percent of the profit, which will also cover the costs of light bites and tea!

LANGUAGE

As a community we are culturally and racially diverse. It's a gift to hold space for different perspectives and experiences because this is where the learning and true connection occurs. Everyone who attends trusts that you'll ensure that their voices are respected and encouraged. On your end, this will require you to be present and observant of the energy moving in conversation. Everyone will be looking to you to keep the energy up, to prompt meaningful questions, and to facilitate their sacred time!

Goddess Council prioritizes assisting women and anyone who identifies as a "goddess" to embrace community as a wellness practice. It's important to avoid using language that's exclusionary when describing our community. As a host, you're the official representative of our organization and overall mission, and it's important to establish acceptable language to be used within gatherings and outside of them. This doesn't need to be overt, but if anything is mentioned within the space that doesn't truly align with our mission, feel free to privately correct any individual or group on their rhetoric.

If you're unsure about someone's pronouns feel free to ask them directly or use their name in conversation.

Goddess Council prides itself on being a community that cultivates safety for everyone's inner goddess to take up space and flourish freely. Most of this is ensured through facilitated productive conversation on your part, but the other part is ushered in through thoughtful ambiance. One of your top goals should be to have every person walk through the door and immediately feel a sense of relief—this usually comes in the form of a deep sigh followed by a smile.

We're truly so excited to have you on board! You are us and we are you, so as you embrace this role as a host, please know that the lines of communication are *always* open. We want feedback and are looking to improve, in all ways. On behalf of your community, thank you!

XO,
Goddess Council

ACKNOWLEDGMENTS

This book is the culmination of the many experiences and life-changing lessons that have been put on my path so far, but it wouldn't have been made possible without the kindness, care, and love of my community.

I want to start off by thanking my dear friend Brad Benson for planting the seed in my mind over a decade ago that one day I'd become an author. When we met, I was a nineteen year old working at Whole Foods and riddled with self-doubt related to what I was meant to do in the world, yet you spoke life into me and made me believe I was meant to triumph over my existential insecurities. I'm not sure what exactly it was that you saw in me at that time, but I am forever indebted to you for encouraging me to believe. I am so grateful for your presence in my life and cherish you more than words can describe.

Guela, thank you for leading a life I am proud to be a witness to. You have dedicated your days to building community, being of service, and loving others, which has inspired me to try my best to always do the same. I feel privileged to be your granddaughter. Te amo.

Tia Evi, thank you for infusing me with affirmations and positivity throughout this process. You never once doubted that I had what it took to transform this idea into the reality I dreamed of. Your assuredness in my abilities oftentimes kept me going throughout the moments doubt crept in. Thank you for existing and for being a light in my life. I love you.

Mami, thank you for cheering me on and having unwavering faith that this could be possible. I love you.

Papi, I hope this project makes you proud. I love you.

Isabella, since the moment you were born, I have lived every day with an awareness that I'm in some way setting an example for you. My lifelong goal has always been to inch closer to embodying the truest version of myself, and my hope is that by never giving up on that mission you are offered proof that writing our own life story is beyond possible. You can be whoever you want to be and do whatever you want, so long as it's in service of your soul's expression. I love you with every molecule that exists in me and will forever adore Soleil as fiercely as I do you.

Amy, not only are you the powerhouse behind Parea Books, but you're the first person in the literary world to ever take a chance on me. When we first began the publishing process, I shared how nervous I was to take up space because of how unconventional my path has been, but your confidence in me and this book immediately washed away any limiting beliefs that lingered within me. You've opened up the doors for me, and now I will never again doubt that my stories and ideas deserve to live out in the open. You've forever changed my life.

Alyea, thank you for being an incredible editor and encouraging my growth as a writer. You're the first editor I've ever worked with and I feel lucky that you chose this project to mold with your expertise and precision. You're incredible at what you do and are helping make dreams come true.

Sending a big hug and thanks to: Frances Baca, Janet Blake, Alissa Dinallo, the Two Rivers Distribution team, the Goddess Council community, Soleil Francois, Skylar Rose Clarke, Jasmine Defrant, Solana Defrant, D'ana Nuñez, Natalie Edgar, Jen Winston, Misako Envela, Elizabeth Perez, Sebastian Perez, Claribel Perez, Alisa Jimenez, and every single person who has played a role in bringing this book to life.

Acknowledgments

If you've made it this far, I want to thank you for deciding to invest in this book and for having faith in me as a writer. I am eternally grateful to you for your belief in me.

ABOUT THE AUTHOR

Cat Lantigua (she/her) is a first-generation Dominican American creative living between Ciudad de Mexico and New York City. Lantigua founded Goddess Council, a global women's wellness collective that operated through 2021 and is the host of the *Chats with Cat* podcast. She is a writer, wellness facilitator, audio producer, and community architect passionate about building spaces that foster soul-centered conversations and a sense of belonging. Cat is a graduate of the Steven J. Green School of International & Public Affairs at Florida International University.

Build It and They Will Come
Cat Lantigua

ISBN 979-8-9885160-2-6

parea
BOOKS

Published by Parea Books
www.pareabooks.com
about@pareabooks.com

Copyright 2024 Cat Lantigua

All rights reserved, including the right of reproduction
in whole or in part in any form.

Every reasonable effort has been made to obtain permission
to include the copyrighted material that appears in this book.
If any rights holder feels that copyrighted material has been
used in error, please contact Parea Books and we will endeavor
to rectify the situation in future books.

EDITOR
Amy Snook and Alyea Canada

PROOFREADER
Janet Blake

COVER DESIGN AND ILLUSTRATION
Alissa Dinallo

INTERIOR DESIGN
Frances Baca

AUTHOR PHOTOGRAPH
Elena Kosharny

Typeset in Eighties Comeback, Skema Pro, and Firm

Printed in Colombia